Sex & Status

Also by Doris Jonas and David Jonas

Man-Child
Young Till We Die
Other Senses, Other Worlds
Primeval Mechanisms
The First Word
Woman and Power (with M. Konig and R. Fester)
The Cave Experience (with R. Fester)

Sex & Status

*Doris Jonas, F.R.A.I.
and David Jonas*

5B
A Scarborough Book
STEIN AND DAY/*Publishers*/New York

FIRST SCARBOROUGH BOOKS EDITION 1980

Sex & Status was originally published in hardcover by
Stein and Day/*Publishers* in 1975.
Copyright © 1974 by Doris Jonas and David Jonas
All rights reserved
Designed by Ed Kaplin
Printed in the United States of America
Stein and Day/*Publishers*/Scarborough House, Briarcliff Manor, N.Y. 10510

Library of Congress Cataloging in Publication Data

Jonas, Doris.

   Sex and status.

   1. Sexual disorders. 2. Social status. 3. Self-
reliance. 4. Social adjustment. I. Jonas, Adolphe
David, 1913-   joint author. II. Title
HQ21.J625   301.41'7   74-23275
ISBN 0-8128-6069-1

Contents

Note

For obvious reasons names and circumstances
have been disguised sufficiently to guard
the privacy of the people concerned without
altering the essence of their accounts.

1

An Introduction

Most of us like to think that mankind is several steps removed from the rest of the animal kingdom, but we are much more biologically controlled than we may care to recognize. This book was written to show that many of our deepest personal problems arise precisely because we so often fail to take into account the basic animal drives that we have inherited from our prehuman ancestors.

Our minds tell us that we can behave reasonably, that as human beings we can think, and so we believe that we can control our destinies. But biologically we still possess strong animal drives; our bodies obey many of the patterns common to all living creatures. We, too, are part of nature, and the laws that govern all living cells, whether plant or animal, are built into the fabric of our being.

The laws that are particularly important to humans are those that govern group behavior, for we are, above all, animals that function best in social groups. Our position within the group, and our ability to adjust to society, to belong, to be accepted are basic to our mental and physical well-being. However, since our cultural development is superimposed on (and often competes with) the old biological laws, we frequently try to flout or manipulate some aspects of them, feeling that we know better.

For instance, we see inequalities in human societies and, because we are human, try to correct them. We know that there are inequalities in other animal groups—hierarchies, dominance rankings, pecking orders—but we think that, being endowed with reason, we ought to be above all that. How far, though, can reason lead us away from life's patterns before we begin to pay a price?

One of the most important aspects of group behavior that this book will discuss is *status*. This is a word that may have many different meanings. It can mean position in society or the prestige attached to position. It can mean a person's position in the family, at work, or in the community, either as seen by the person, or by others, or by the group as a whole. Status can mean any or all of these things, and this book will use the term in these senses, but it will also, and chiefly, examine status as it applies in most animal groups—that is, the quality possessed by those that function efficiently within their group. In this sense, status in mankind is manifested by an inner feeling of confidence. Its possessor has a sense of self-worth and satisfaction, a sense that ultimately leads to the glorious feeling of being a success.

We do not always use the word *status* in its conventional sense of high-ranking social position. Although achievement of social position is often the result of a person's inner feeling of self-worth, sometimes it is not. For instance, in a business organization occupying a large building there may be an executive whom the world views as holding a high position. However, if there are circumstances in his life that erode his self-confidence, his inner feelings will not correspond to the high position in which the world sees him. In the same building there may be a cleaning woman who does excellent work and is often praised for it. She is proud of her shining floors and tidy rooms and thinks she is as good as the best cleaner anywhere. In the conventional sense it seems that the executive holds higher status than the cleaning woman, but in their inmost feelings she has a sense of standing while he does not. These inner feelings in the long run determine biological function in general and sexual function in particular.

Among animals other than man, those who have this sense of success are the natural leaders; they take on the roles of perpetuating and protecting their kind. They are the breeders. It is in this sense that this book will speak of sex: the ability to form bonds and to breed.

Like status, the word *sex* has many denotations. It can mean the sexual act, reproduction, or gender. All these things are part of sex, and this book will talk about them all in turn. But its widest theme is how the various aspects of sex are related to an individual's status—his self-confidence, or sense of success as a living creature. Animals that do not have this sense of status in their groups may form a standby reserve or may eventually be eliminated from the group. Usually, at least so long as a dominant individual is present, they do not breed.

The thought of applying these principles to ourselves is abhorrent to us. We feel that all human beings who are born and survive have a right to a place in society, to form bonds, and to reproduce themselves. We use every means at our disposal to retain in our ranks the less well-adapted along with the well-adapted; those who in biological terms one might call "failures" along with the "successes." Ironically, the penalties of this practice are felt by the very people we attempt to protect. Despite the good intentions of others, the less well-adapted often are socially ill at ease, lack self-confidence, gain little satisfaction in life, feel they lack competence, and in a general sense they lack standing, rank, or status among their peers.

The feeling of being a loser, a social failure, can lead to all kinds of malfunctions that begin with the individual but affect ever-widening circles until the society as a whole is disturbed. The society then must care for those who suffer the consequences of the social failure's sense of insecurity and stress. The ramifications of these feelings can be found in frightened adolescents, unhappy marriages, broken homes, sexual deviance, illness, impotence, and frigidity.

Who among us, at first glance, would connect the manifestation of, say, impotence, with the natural working of social groups? Experts have always regarded it as an individual problem, whether medical or psychological. But it is really much more basic than that; impotence stems from a feeling of failure first within the family group and then, because of that first failure, a subsequent failure to adapt to the social group in adulthood.

If we want to redress some of the ills that arise from this sense of failure and give any real help to those who suffer from it, we have to look at the natural process as a whole. We have to see what aggressiveness, the will to dominate, to fight for rank and status within a group, or the absence of these drives actually means in the larger picture of the social group, as well as to the individual concerned.

In every group, whether human or nonhuman, hierarchy (which implies status) plays a regulatory role. Some people compete aggressively for top place; some find a niche at a lower level and exist in it quite happily; some cannot accept the place they are assigned and struggle to improve it. Some move up in this struggle, some lose. If a person's accepted place is lowered, he or she will show the effect: problems will ensue. Even though mankind as a species is one of the few that on the whole looks after its weak, and is the only one that does so extensively, the old responses are still within us. All human beings need to feel that they are accepted by their social group. We hate to lose, to fail, to go down in rank or self-esteem.

This book is concerned with discovering how much we can do to help our "losers" readjust to society and rehabilitate themselves. But we must first understand the workings of social groups, so that we can know how our maladjusted came to feel the way they do.

This book is sparked primarily by a desire to bring real and effective help to people who suffer from all kinds of sexual difficulties, overt or covert. Until now these problems have been handled piecemeal, as either medical or psychological difficulties. Although medical and psychological symptoms are often present, dealing with these alone is not sufficiently helpful. Accepted theories of sexual problems may be valid so far as the individual is concerned, but they do not explain why mankind should be the only species subject to these malfunctions.

The subject of sex and status has many facets. To deal with it exhaustively would require a prolonged study of mankind's history, a Herculean task. But to see human sexual problems as the fallout of natural group processes will nevertheless require examining one aspect of evolutionary development after another until we see the overall design. It is like looking at something familiar and finding in it a feature so basic that it has hitherto been overlooked. As the design emerges we find new understanding, and with understanding comes the possibility of giving effective help.

The easiest way to come to this understanding is by going back to simpler animal societies and seeing how they work—how they are held together, how they ensure sufficient numbers and qualities to endure as a group. Sometimes it is startling to see that a characteristic we think of as purely human is actually found throughout nature. We are so dazzled by the external trappings of man's culture that we don't always see the basic trends, common to all living things, that lie beneath them. We may gasp at the beauty of a piece of jewelry, admire the art of its designer, and boggle at the king's ransom it costs. We don't really stop to think about its chief function, which is not to adorn but to assert rank. In this it is in no way different from the little bits of leaves, petals, pebbles, and odds and ends with which a bowerbird decorates his bower. He, too, is providing adornment and thereby asserting his rank. Seeing these group mechanisms at work in other creatures, it is far easier to identify them in ourselves and recognize the purposes they serve.

2

Sex and Status

When a socially successful or very rich man marries an attractive younger woman, cynics, gossipmongers, friends, and strangers are apt to think that the young woman is only interested in his wealth and position—in fact, that she is a "gold digger"—and that the rich man is foolish in his choice, for the match will be unrewarding and costly to him.

The successful man is not always rich. His success may be in the arts, in public affairs, or in almost any walk of life; regardless of his personal or physical qualities, he attracts young and desirable women. Many examples of these so-called May-and-December marriages pique our interest. A world-famous painter, an acclaimed cellist, a Supreme Court justice, a motion picture immortal, billionaire shipowners and industrialists—all have married women young enough to be their daughters or granddaughters, and not all of these young women are Lorelei Lees.

On the other side, we all know there are men who either are unsuccessful in their fields, or have been successful but have suffered setbacks, who always seem to be rejected by all but the most maternal women. These men lose interest in their mates, and often in women in general. They complain that women are only interested in men for the material advantages they can get from them, that women do not care for men at all except for their money and prestige, and that women are castrating harpies. Yet in their less bitter moments these men, as well as the rest of us, know that this is not the case. Very few, if any, women are such total monsters as a Philip Wylie, or Edward Albee, or Philip

Roth would have them—any more than men are irredeemable brutes.

Yet it is true that the status of a man or woman has a profound impact on his or her sexual being, and this book will explore one of the basic mechanisms that lie beneath the sexual drive, or lack of it, the chief ingredient in every individual's success or lack of success in male-female relationships.

In the course of the development of any species, natural selection tends to preserve individuals who carry traits that are advantageous to their species' survival. So, at any given time in the life of a species, we can assume that the characteristics we find in it either serve, or in the course of the species' history have served, some purpose useful to its survival. Often we attribute characteristics of behavior, or ideals that people believe in, to the particular culture in which we find them. But invariably when we look a little closer we find that behavior and ideals are the outcome of the biological raw material that has become transmuted into the bricks and mortar of the structure of the culture. That is, people do not behave in a certain way only because of the culture they grew up in, but also because the culture itself grew around habits and attitudes that were biologically carried in the people because they were useful.

It is now generally known that it is not possible to inherit habits or behavior as such. Nevertheless the ability or potential to act in a certain way is inherited, and there is a tendency for this potential for "useful" behavior to be preserved in the genetic endowment of a group.

Evolutionary processes on the whole have worked in a direction toward the dominant members of social groups becoming the chief progenitors of the next generation. (This is a very general statement that applies in varying degrees and modifications in different species, and a later chapter will describe how this comes about.) Therefore the attainment of dominance and the hormonal outpourings that are preliminary to mating are strongly tied together. And, as a concomitant, failure to attain dominance and inhibition of those hormonal secretions are also tied together.

This sounds like a very effective procedure to ensure that a society is chiefly populated by the progeny of its successful individuals, while its unsuccessful are eliminated through lack of issue. But a society populated by the offspring of successful, dominant individuals is more likely to survive in the long run, while a society with too many misfits will be eliminated. This happens automatically in nature, and it is the essence of the process that goes by the name of natural selection.

In the case of man just as much as in other species, the successful person, whether male or female, always finds it easy to acquire a mate of his or her own choosing even if he or she, to outward appearances, is too old or too ugly. What constitutes success, of course, varies not only among cultures but also among different groups within a culture, and even among individuals within a group. It may consist of wealth, whether in terms of money, land, or herds; it may consist of high achievement, whether in scholarship, art, or profession; it may be in personal attributes, whether of beauty, leadership, or athletic skills. Whatever the areas of success, the important part is that the person *feels* successful and, because of this feeling, acquires a certain charisma that conveys the feeling to others.

The connection between sexual performance and a sense of status goes even further than the physical act itself. In the days when a girl's chastity and a woman's fidelity were highly prized, a suitor who was cheated or a husband who was cuckolded was considered, and felt himself to be, extremely ridiculous. The infidelity implied that his lady found his masculinity deficient. The comedy of the playwrights of the Restoration period in England often hinged on such situations. Molière, too, used them to point up the vanities of the fashionable world, as have many other playwrights in other countries and at other times.

Nor is this a one-sided matter. A woman whose husband is unfaithful is hurt or angry not only because his action seems to show that he does not love her, but also because it implies that her femininity is not sufficient to hold him. She believes her status relative to other women (or another woman) is lowered, and her feelings for herself and for the man are wounded. Oddly enough this situation, also the subject of great literature, is usually treated as drama and not as comedy. Perhaps this is because the writers until recent times were usually male, and they did not identify themselves so strongly with the jilted woman as they did with the cuckolded man. The jilted woman was not funny in their eyes. She was a Fury, Revenge personified, or merely a pitiful object who pined away. It is clear that these are images of how the man experienced her and not of how she felt about herself.

An extension of this theme, but its converse, was the ancient custom of assessing a man according to the number of women who were his, whose existence in his household attested to his virility. King Solomon had "seven hundred wives, princesses, and three hundred concubines," and he "clave unto these in love," and therefore obviously was a great man, even for a king. Today, in lands where polygamy is permitted, a ruler still surrounds himself with a host of women, no matter how decrepit or impotent he may be. He may or may not derive pleasure from them, but through them he asserts his virility and cements his status.

The female's equivalent of this display is to win the love of famous men and subject them to her charms and whims. Thus Cleopatra's name resounds through history because she commanded the devotion of Caesar and of Antony, rather than because of her achievements as a queen. Helen of Troy is supreme among women because kings and armies fought to possess her: it was not her achievements that motivated them, but her femininity.

At this point it is not hard to imagine a chorus of objections: this or that great leader or well-known personality had sexual problems, or was indifferent to sex. Of course, much of what we know about the great and near-great is anecdotal. Really to understand their personal inclinations, we should have to know much more than we usually do about their private lives and feelings. A classical example of this kind of myth is the case of Hitler. He has been presented as an "abstemious celibate who abjured elaborate foods, women, and sex." But his recent biographer, Robert Payne, writes that this image was for the German public. In fact, he claims, "Hitler loved cakes and candy, he exerted his Viennese charm on the ladies around him and he had various mistresses throughout his public career." Since nothing arises out of a vacuum it is quite possible that the myth of his abstemiousness arose out of his early life, when he was a social failure. His paintings, mediocre as they were, met with no acceptance, and he led a borderline existence. At that stage in his life he was known to be uninterested in sex. It could well be that this image later on suited his purposes and he made a virtue out of the earlier failing. It was only after he received the adulation, respect, and standing that went with the power he attained later in life that he acquired mistresses and finally publicly acknowledged his romance with Eva Braun.

There is a universal recognition of the close connection between strong sexuality and high status, even if we do not customarily think of them in this way. What this book is concerned with is why this is so: what is the actual physical basis of this connection, and how much does it influence the personal life of every one of us?

The possession of high standing in any field seems to enhance virility in man. United States Commerce Secretary Peter Peterson often quotes his friend Henry Kissinger as saying, "Peterson, you wouldn't have any way of knowing this, but power is the ultimate aphrodisiac." It is commonly accepted that people who achieve fame or notoriety are sought by the opposite sex, and are biologically "at the ready" for sex. What we do not recognize is that it is also normal for the unsuccessful person to be biologically "turned off." He is not revved up to go. On the contrary, his hormonal apparatus is tuned down to adjust him to submission. But, not recognizing this, we expect such a person to function sexually as though he were a dominant individual, and neither we nor he can understand it when he encounters difficulties.

It seems inconceivable to us that for some people to be "turned down" or even "turned off" is as natural as for others to be "turned on." What is more, the victim himself does not understand why he cannot function readily in an area he has been taught to believe is natural and pleasureful. While he may realize that he has suffered defeat in one area of life, he does not connect this in his mind with so-called natural functions like sex. On the contrary, modern men on the whole are aware that much is expected of them. Any difficulty in fulfilling these expectations accentuates their feeling of defeat, enlarges their problem, and leads to psychological disorders.

While we are talking here about males because of their more active biological function in the mating process, the same mechanisms also apply to females. The so-called pecking order, by which we first recognized the rank stratification of animal populations, was observed among barnyard hens, and hierarchical order was later observed among the females of many other species. A woman's feeling of self-worth and rank relate more closely to acquiring a mate than to adequacy in actual mating. This, of course, works out to the same end result, for if a female does not acquire a mate, she provides her population with no progeny—any more than does the male who is an ineffective mate.

In our own societies, many a girl feels that only a successful (desirable, attractive, strong, or whatever the value that prevails in her group) female can hope to attain a desirable male. For the female, too, recognition in one area can outweigh what appear to be disadvantages, or even disqualifications, in others. Lack of beauty, poor health, a domineering father, and Victorian mores, for example, did not prevent Elizabeth Barrett from winning the love of the young, handsome, and successful Robert Browning. Her confidence in her worth as a poet attracted him to her and eventually united them in one of the world's favorite love stories. Alma Gropius Mahler Werfel provides another outstanding example of a woman whose status enhanced her sexually. She was certainly an intelligent, charming, and attractive woman, but there were surely quite a few others in the Viennese society of her time possessed of the same qualities. It was her own confidence in herself as a woman (her female status) that propelled her into the company of eminent men and eventually resulted in three marriages, each with a man of world-acknowledged talent who was supreme in his own field in his time.

Another woman who has long captured the imagination of those who know of her was Lou Andreas-Salomé. She was adored by Nietzsche, became the mistress of Rilke, may have been the cause of Paul Rée's suicide, was loved by Victor Tausk, and may have been responsible for his self-mutilation and suicide. She is known by a wider circle as a friend, student, and disciple of Freud who was allowed to enter his circle of close confidantes. She became a friend of Anna Freud and was a practicing lay analyst. An enjoyable biography written of her by H. F. Peters leaves one wondering what incredible charms this woman possessed. She clearly had a quality of personality that attracted the intellectual giants of her time, men who memorialized their loves in art and writing and through whom we know of her. Other women with similar qualities have certainly existed, but because they attracted men who left no record, their lives and loves remain unknown to us.

If a woman lacks confidence in herself—if she feels that her attributes place her in a low rank—this very feeling intensifies the condition and contributes even further to her self-disqualification. She too is aware of her society's expectation that she should meet young men, that they should find her interesting and exciting, that she should eventually find a mate from among them. Parents and friends may urge her to go out in company, to find a "date," to marry, or whatever; it is equally possible that the pressure exists only in her own mind. But, in either case, if she feels unqualified this feeling becomes a disabling factor, reducing her rank in her own eyes. The ensuing feeling of defeat then contributes to her malfunctioning as a female.

It would seem that what we are actually pointing out—that a person who is successful in one area, and so has a general sense of confidence about his standing within his social group, is likely also to be successful as a sexual being—is rather obvious. Folk wisdom has provided us with aphorisms like "success breeds success" that state the matter very succinctly. Yet many things that we take for granted prove to be marvels of interlocking causes and mechanisms when observed closely. We have only to look at slow-motion pictures of a taken-for-granted movement like walking to see that it is in fact a wonderful synthesis of almost incredible complexity.

Even more complex are mankind's attitudes and responses in sexual behavior, including the particular facet of it that relates to status. We are, after all, sexual beings, and almost every aspect of our lives is in some way related to that fact. Probably for this reason everything that pertains to sexuality has enormous fascination for us, and the more obvious aspects of this drive have been investigated time and again. But status is one of the mechanisms of sexuality that most people consider more remote from the breeding function, and it has been passed by. It is usually not thought of as a part of nature's pattern of genetic devices at all.

Status does not only affect interpersonal relationships; the sense of rank is an intrinsic part of the mechanical responses in the physical act of sex. A confident feeling can be a trigger, and a depressed and/or embarrassed feeling an inhibitor of sexual function. In many cases, if not most, such difficulties as partial or total impotence and frigidity are inextricably entwined with a person's feelings about his or her own standing.

Indeed, over and above its purely reproductive function, sex plays a very special role in the life of mankind, as we shall see.

3

Man's Supersexuality

In the rest of the animal world, sexual activity bears some relationship to the needs of animal populations to regenerate themselves. Excessive numbers of young are produced by all species, and these numbers are then thinned out by predators, by accident, by the availability of food supply, and by other means, so that on the whole only the best-adapted strains survive. Just the same, the sexual life of the adult animal is geared to reproduction. Sex is a periodic or seasonal preoccupation. Mating invariably takes place at a time when, allowing time for gestation, the young resulting from it will have the best chance for survival. In many species, adults are almost asexual the rest of the time.

In man this is not the case. There is no season, no day, no hour when it is not possible for human beings to mate, and children may be born at any time of the year. For such striking modification of a general pattern there has to be a reason.

The chief characteristic that differentiates man from other animals is our special brain, and the development of this brain and of our ability to use it is made possible by our long period of growth, development, and learning in childhood. The greatest amount of brain growth (as much as seventy-five percent of it) takes place in the first three years of our lives, when we are at our most helpless, and if there were not a very strong bond to hold our parents together so that they could share the burdens of caring for us, we could hardly have survived, either as individuals or as a species. Prolonged sexuality has been a large factor in forging those bonds.

Among primates the family pattern as we know it is not unique to man. The gibbons, too, form strong pair bonds. They stay together in families that comprise a male, a female, and their offspring, and the young remain with their parents until they are mature, as ours do. This would indicate that nonseasonal sexuality is not the only factor in cementing family ties, but it is nevertheless a powerful one. Because of it, feelings that accompany the sexual act have a chance to become extended into love and concern for the other, and this forms the best possible atmosphere for our young to reach their full potential. Therefore it can fairly be said that, in spite of the disapproval with which our Victorian ancestors regarded it, man's year-round and prolonged sexuality was to some extent an instrument in our evolution as a species. To put this a little more scientifically, a high degree of sexuality gave a selective advantage to those who possessed it.

It goes without saying that in this, as in almost all the mechanisms of life, there is a complex intertwining between cause and effect. That parents stay together and divide the labors necessary to care for a child promotes the welfare of the child. But a child who has been lovingly cared for will develop responses that will incline it, in turn, to give care to others when it is an adult.

A newborn child is rather an inert creature, unable to move from place to place or to perceive its surroundings very clearly. The first stimuli its nervous system receives from the outside world are the fondling, cradling, and handling of its mother as she feeds it, cleans it, and carries it in her arms. The human being is not alone in this: ape and monkey mothers handle, feed, and groom their young; mother cats use their tongues to clean and caress theirs; and so, or similarly, do many other animals. But the human baby's long helplessness requires intensification of this kind of care, so that while its nervous system is developing and growing at its most rapid pace, it is doing so largely in response to the stimulation of the millions of tiny nerve endings in the skin. This type of fondling becomes an essential element in the development of the nervous system's response mechanisms, and the nervous system never forgets it.

We have learned from laboratory experiments how profoundly the natural lives of apes can be deformed by isolating them from contact with their mothers. How much more devastating, then, is the effect of similar sterile rearing on the human baby, who is so much more helpless for so much longer. Normally, of course, a baby receives at least some measure of the ministrations it needs, and in this way a whole set of responses becomes established in the brain. The nervous system learns to react to bodily intimacy, and when the child grows up it is, so to speak, preconditioned to seeking and giving bodily contact, which offers its most intense gratification in the wide range of sexual expression.

Thus sex in man has become more than a drive to procreate. It has become a means of achieving an intense pleasure, which is sought for its own sake. And here we have the closing of the circle: the sexuality that binds the parents and enables them to give care of a special order to their child results in a prolonged stimulation of the child's nervous system, so that it in turn becomes an adult highly responsive to tenderness and to close bodily contacts, and with a capacity for a high degree of sexuality.

It is interesting that man's nearest relatives, the chimpanzees, are only periodically sexual in the wild, but in zoos (as Desmond Morris has pointed out) they, like man, mate at any time of the year. It would seem that when the chimpanzee is denied the activities that are normal in its natural habitat, its energies are displaced into sexual activity. (Man responds in a similar way. Nine months after the power failure that caused a prolonged blackout in New York, preventing people from going about their usual occupations, an unusually high number of births was recorded.) The significance of supersexuality in captive chimpanzees for us, though, is that it indicates that the *potential* for year-round sexual drive is present in them too and must also have been present as a potential in our common ancestors and in the main primate line. This potential, coming to fruition in man, has been a factor in making it possible for us to develop, as we have, the full complement of attributes we regard as "human," including our vast intelligence.

So the human being is a supersexual creature! Many readers, male and female alike, may object to this generalization on the basis of their personal experience—the experiences of all the wives who feel frustrated by their husbands' coldness and all the husbands who feel that their wives are too often "too tired." Others may simply respond, "You must be joking." And there is indeed a whole literature of jokes about a spouse's lack of responsiveness. Indirectly, such jokes offer support to the thesis that man is hypersexual, for they reveal the feeling that a deficiency in this quality *should* not exist. When it does, the results are frustration, anger, impatience, and/or sullen with-drawal.

Man's hypersexuality is in some ways similar to his intelligence. There is no denying that a high degree of intelligence is one of the hallmarks of our species. Yet there is a wide range between the most and the least intelligent of us that is called normal, and at each end of the spectrum there are the extremes that we call genius and dull-to-defective. That a large number of us fall into the dull-to-de-fective category does not invalidate the statement that man is an intelligent species. It is significant that there is as large a body of jokes and folklore about low intelligence as there is about low sexuality.

In tribal societies a common method of dealing with those who indulge in deviant behavior is ridicule. Ridicule is more effective than any law or punishment in keeping behavior conformative, because it is a weapon that erodes both the respect of others and self-respect and therefore demolishes the person's importance in his community. The fear of ridicule is ingrained. We can see it in our own children ("Don't laugh at me"), and we have to teach them ways of dealing with it to protect their self-esteem. One of the devices we use is to handle ridicule with good humor, to make a joke of the "insult"—actually, not to accept it as meant to be true.

Because we find that people universally treat low intelligence and poor sexual performance as subjects for joking, we must recognize that there is everywhere a feeling that it is demeaning to be regarded as deficient in these areas. We feel that a loss of status is associated with this kind of inadequacy—a loss of status so painful that we can only cope with it by laughing it off.

Considered objectively, sexual desire is essential not to individual survival, but only to species survival, as opposed to drives like hunger and thirst, which unquestionably serve the individual. On this basis it might be thought that appetite should be felt to be more central than sex, and yet this is not the way we feel. Loss of appetite is not accompanied by feelings of inferiority or inadequacy. We feel free to talk about it without a trace of embarrassment, whereas reduction or loss of sexual drive makes us feel *less*. This feeling alone is a clue and confirmation of the special place of sex among the vital drives.

Of course, in the whole animal world it is not possible to exagger-ate the important role of sex. It determines body structure, fixes separate roles, and seasonally pervades the totality of a creature's functions, in some even to the detriment of self-preservation. But, the mating season past, sex does not affect the day-to-day, year-round behavior of other animals as it does that of man. For man, the possessor of a special kind of brain, sex goes beyond the satisfaction of an urgent drive. Even when its primary needs are satisfied, sex doesn't fade away as do thoughts of food when hunger is satisfied, but persists on many conscious and subconscious levels.

Other animals may copulate beyond the actual necessities for reproduction, either with the same or several partners. But they do this only during a limited season. For the rest of the time they are preoccupied with satisfying their hunger drive more than their sexual one.

As for us, we also enjoy food beyond the necessities of satisfying hunger. Perhaps this arises from the close association of food with the love and care and handling of our mothers in our earliest memories, so that for many of us food may be equated with love. Indeed, for some people food takes the place of sex. The need for loving attention is so compelling that if it is not satisfied in one area it demands gratification in another.

Man's supersexuality is not just a matter of being open to sexual stimulus at any time of the year. It is subtly, and sometimes not so subtly, manifested in activities where it would seem to be completely irrelevant. A man may hire an assistant because he finds her appealing, irrespective of her capacity to perform the job he wants done. A woman may dress herself attractively, perhaps seductively, when she has not the slightest idea of forming any close relationship with the men she meets or even if she does not expect to meet any men at all. Painting, sculpture, literature, music, dance, all are permeated with sexual connotations. Even man's technology intensifies an already intense preoccupation with sex, since technology promotes leisure, and leisure has gone hand in hand with sexual indulgence and the arts that embellish it from time immemorial. It seems that as soon as mankind is relieved of the need to sustain itself by hard work, the ever-present capacity to respond sexually flourishes in myriad forms of pure pleasure.

Historically, the greatest excesses of decadent luxury were concerned with heightening the possibilities for sexual response. In the rich civilization of ancient Egypt, women of the highest class wore clothing of transparent fabrics and adorned their bodies with cosmetics, their rouged nipples showing through their gowns. With the wealth of the known world pouring into Rome, relieving many people of the necessity to labor, indulgence of the senses reached new heights. Suetonius recorded:

> Not satisfied with seducing freeborn boys and married women, Nero raped the Vestal Virgin Rubria. . . . Having tried to turn the boy Sporus into a girl by castration, he went through a wedding ceremony with him, dowry, bridal veil and all. . . . He was released from a den dressed in the skins of wild animals, and attacked the private parts of men and women who stood bound to stakes. After working up sufficient excitement by this means he was despatched—shall we say?—by his freedman Doryphorus. Doryphorus now married him—just as he himself had married Sporus—and on the wedding night he imitated the screams and moans of a girl being deflowered.

In the court of Louis XIV, when France was at its height of power and wealth, sexual indulgence again reached excess. And even today, what is the purpose of our multi–billion-dollar cosmetic industry? And of the advertising profession that suffuses automobiles, household products, tobacco, and alcohol with sexual overtones? What the advertising men understand, without perhaps knowing why, is simply that in our species male and female alike can be influenced through their sexuality even more than through their instinct for survival.

Besides these obvious ways in which our species' immense sexual potential is expressed, there are less blatant ways in which aspects of our being that essentially have little to do with our sexuality are nevertheless incorporated into it.

In a very real way all our senses, especially those of touch and feeling but also those of seeing, smelling, and hearing, have become tributaries of our sexuality—so much so that in our thoughts the terms *sensuality* and *sexuality* are closely interwoven. This is not so for other creatures. While a visual signal, sound, or odor may be the spark that sets their sexual apparatus into operation, these senses, so far as we know, play no part in their coital experience. For us, though, the comfort of physical closeness, the pleasures of touching and feeling are almost inseparable from sex. We might say that our sexuality has engulfed a large part of our sensuality.

In the rest of the animal kingdom, a creature's sexual activity is totally dependent upon its hormonal production, but this is not the case with us. A woman who has had her uterus, ovaries, or both removed is able to feel love and respond sexually as strongly as she could before. The same applies to a woman past menopause, when her level of hormone production is drastically reduced. That the loss of one or both testicles has a more devastating effect on a man is probably more due to social values than to an actual loss of desire.

On the other hand, an absence of sexual desire for whatever reason cannot be remedied by taking hormones. Man's sexuality is so diffused throughout his being that it is no longer dependent upon the production of hormones. It is brought into play by associations and memories, by the comforts of closeness and of long habit, by the imagination working through sights and sounds, by the excitement of intellectual compatibility. Any such stimulus, working through the nervous system, may produce a sexual response in men and women at any time in any season and at whatever age.

This is the point where, as a rule, investigations into man's sexuality stop, and it has the effect of making of sex an isolated phenomenon—an entity of itself. But if we look at sex as a social function, one that is at the service of the group, or species, as well as of the individual, then we have to place it into the broader context. To do this requires a good look at the matter of status.

4

The Drive for Status
in General

Man has many vital drives, and various psychologists have focused on one or another of them in their attempts to find a basic motivation for our behavior. Freud focused on sex, Adler on the drive for power, Jung on innate feelings of continuity with the past.

Of all the drives motivating man, the drive for status—rank, dominance, call it what you will—is probably the most overlooked in attempting to find an overall explanation for our behavior. Although Adler's ideas on the drive for power came close, he attributed this drive to a need to compensate for the powerlessness of infancy and failed to consider the struggle for dominance in animal groups.

The drive for rank both predates and outlasts the sex drive. Its fulfillment may not be quite so vital to an individual as the satisfaction of hunger, but it probably ranks next as a constituent of a person's feelings of well-being. The contest for dominance begins in earliest childhood (in some degree even in babyhood), and colors all phases of adult life; in old age, the retention of status acquired in adult life is the most important ingredient in feelings of the "worthwhileness" of living.

It seems puzzling that something so obvious as the inclination to seek and acknowledge status should have been noticed by so few, and then only tangentially, in the matter of sex. Perhaps just because it is so all-pervasive in our daily lives, we take status for granted and give it little more thought than breathing. Some aspects of status do come up from time to time: sibling rivalry, for example, causes problems for not a few parents, and ways to cope with it are often discussed, but its deeper significance is rarely considered. For the human mother does not see this kind of rivalry as a perfectly natural contest for status among her children, but as a nuisance that makes life difficult for her. Unlike the lioness, who looks on unperturbed while her cubs fight to establish their ranking order, the human parent doesn't see this contest as an essential part of her child's development. As a matter of fact, most of us display mixed feelings toward the struggle for rank even though we are at all times involved in it.

Much human competition is ritualized. We usually do not fight or kill a neighbor in order to gain, for example, the food supplies he commands, but we compete with him for them with symbolic weapons: money, intelligence, physical skills and attributes, and the manipulation of influence.

If a man tries to buy tickets for a hit show and is told that none is available, he may mention that he is a relative of the producer and get a pair of house seats. His business friend or female acquaintance is then impressed with his ability to obtain what is unobtainable for all other comers, and his social status in their eyes (as well as in his own) is enhanced.

A diamond jewel is not necessarily prettier than one made of glass, nor is a sable coat necessarily prettier or warmer than one of rabbit fur. But the woman who wears the diamond and sable is accorded a deference not shown to one who wears glass beads and rabbit fur.

School children are encouraged to achieve a high place in their classes, and if successful they are rewarded with praise or prizes. Adults in the business world compete for high-ranking positions and in the professions for standing in their fields. In political life the contest for power is undisguised, even though certain conventions prevail. In all this we are in step with the rest of the animal world, where striving for rank is also ritualized and universal. Mixed feelings arise, especially in the democracies of the Western world, when our ideals of egalitarianism incline us to downgrade ambition and competition.

In some societies rank is accepted as a part of social life, and a person holding rank has no qualms about asserting it, but in ours any overt display is frowned on. We encourage young people to strive for eminence, but teach them not to boast. This dichotomy is more characteristic of Britons than of Americans, and Mediterraneans hardly know it.

But ideals of equality are totally antibiological. In higher and lower animals, in insects, and even in plants, the smaller and weaker die off or are systematically eliminated.

A photographer of animals in the wild has described how the eagle feeds its young with its head up and does not bend down toward them as many other birds do. As a result only the eaglets that stretch up high can reach the food. Their strength, aggressiveness, and competitive spirit are rewarded in a way that adds to their advantage in successive feedings.

Size at birth, or an early spurt in size soon after birth, is often a factor in determining an animal's rank and even its survival. A classic demonstration of this was given in 1958 by Christina M. Richards, who found that large tadpoles of the species *Rana pipiens,* when sufficiently crowded, produce something that powerfully inhibits or arrests the growth of small tadpoles. In further experiments she discovered that the guts and feces of crowded large tadpoles develop enormous quantities of peculiar cells that are not present in uncrowded ones, and that as these cells are passed into the water and accumulate at the bottom they are reingested along with food and act increasingly to inhibit growth. Thus, when a tadpole population is too great for a given volume of water, those with an early size advantage survive, while the others are stunted and die off.

The same principle applies to plant life as well. The smaller seedlings in a pot (which limits the available quantity of soil and space for root growth) do not grow unless the larger ones are removed. You can demonstrate this for yourself. Try planting all the pits of the same ripe grapefruit in a pot. Soon you will see that one or two of them grow taller and stronger than the rest. If you leave them as they are, the strong, fast-growing seedlings will "take over," and the competition for amenities will be between them only. But if you remove the tallest and strongest from the pot, one or two of the others will develop and grow large and strong in their turn.

This preservation of the stronger or larger individuals of a generation at the expense of the weaker or smaller ones is one of the most fundamental mechanisms for the preservation, health, and adjustment of any species. Man's ideal of preserving equally all who are born is, so far as the survival of the species is concerned, actually an anti-ideal.

This idea, of course, is shocking to most people in Western democratic societies. We like to consider our ideas to be an advance on the "law of the jungle," although in recent years, as the remarkable order of animal groups has become apparent to us, a few have had second thoughts. We have to recognize that even in the most "idealistically" egalitarian groups a ranking order, if not an outright hierarchy, inevitably arises. Even if all individuals were born with equal attributes, which they are not, the simple fact that there are always more individuals than positions of prestige available ensures that some attain those positions while others cannot.

The contest for status, although an all-pervading element in our daily lives, is sometimes carried on by subtle means and camouflaged weapons, as the following example shows.

Two sisters of strong personality were married and led separate personal lives, but were partners in business. The younger had worked before her marriage and continued to do so afterward. The older had only begun to work after her marriage, so when she joined the firm she was at a disadvantage in terms of experience. Therefore, although the sisters were equal partners, the employees were inclined to regard the younger as the boss. This disturbed the older. She began to complain to her family, eventually asserting that her sister's treatment of her was the cause of her many physical ailments. The younger sister was troubled by this, but whenever she tried to give the older one more responsibility the older would say, "Oh, don't ask me about that. You know it all much better."

This situation finally became intolerable not only for both sisters, but also for their husbands, their grown children, and their in-laws. When it was pointed out to the sisters that they were actually engaged in a power struggle over the leadership of the firm, they could not believe it. They were not aware that they were engaged in a battle.

In this family we can see a subtle competition for rank. The younger sister used the weapons of efficiency and experience to gain leadership. The older demanded deference to her suffering, which put her in the dominant position when it came to receiving attention. In an animal society such contests are waged with conventional weapons that both parties use, and a result is arrived at. These sisters, each using her own weapons in a conflict with no ground rules, could not come to a decision, and perpetual battle, painful to each of them, was the result.

When each of the contestants chooses a different weapon, it is often difficult for outsiders, too, to recognize the nature of their struggle. The two partners of a textile dyeing company were a good instance of this. One of them prided himself on being a Hard-Headed Businessman, the other on being the proverbial Good Fellow. The HHB believed that sentiment played no part in business, that outlays and receipts, profits and losses were the only things that counted. The GF believed that being affable, helpful, and popular brought in customers and established good relations with workers. Since their workers were largely of non-English-speaking origin, GF made it a practice to visit them in their homes and give them help when they encountered major problems. He also went out of his way to render services to his customers. When it came to dismissing old or inefficient employees, there were always heated disputes between the partners, as could be expected. But when it came to deciding which of them was to represent the firm at important business conferences, the competition between them began to show.

It emerged that GF was using his goodness, as much as HHB was using his pragmatism, as a weapon to prove his business abilities, to such an extent that it was becoming detrimental to the firm as well as to their personal lives. When it was pointed out to them that the actual nature of their differences was competition for the Number One spot in their firm, they were both shocked. Fortunately they came to realize that they had to define their respective functions in the organization with clear boundaries and no overlapping, so that competition between them could not occur. They were then able to direct their natural competitive drives where they could prove useful: against other companies.

Another thread in the complex web of the status drive can be discerned when a man has attained whatever he set out to accomplish in his life, feels adequate in his occupation and likes it, but is then pushed by the ambitions of others to attempt higher levels.

Chris and Jane had been married about twelve years. In that time Chris had advanced to the level his skills as a draftsman permitted. He then settled into that niche quite happily. He was doing what he liked; his employers were satisfied with him; he got on well with his colleagues; he had no further ambitions.

Chris's only relative was an elderly widowed mother, who felt proud of the standing he had gained. Jane, however, came from a large family. Many of her relatives were quite well off and lived in a more lavish style than Chris's salary permitted. In the early years of their marriage Jane had hoped that Chris would eventually become an engineer and reach the top rank in his company, but as she saw him settling into his draftsman's niche she became more and more dissatisfied. She said that she felt ashamed of their apartment: it was not as large nor as well furnished as her sisters', and their address was one from which she hoped to move. She began to nag Chris, cried, and made scenes. She sometimes went so far as to try to manipulate his career behind his back. She canvassed her family connections for a better job for him, faced him with appointments for interviews that she had made on his behalf, and tried to persuade him to go into business on his own. Chris felt very uncomfortable about all this, but from time to time, just to appease her, he made halfhearted attempts to look into the opportunities she brought him.

As Jane came to realize that his efforts were not sincere she became abusive. She told Chris that he was nothing but a lackey; his bosses took advantage of him; he was working overtime and didn't get extra pay. Until then he had not let her prodding disturb him, but with this she got to him. She had found the one place where he was vulnerable—his belief in his status—and he reacted violently. The time came when he actually hit her, and he felt very bad about it. He began to dislike his job. He got into quarrels with his coworkers. At times he became moody and would not talk to anybody. He lost interest in sex. "The idea of it makes me feel sick," he said. After one provocation he hit her harder than usual, she filed a complaint against him, and they ended up in family court, where the judge ordered counseling.

In the family therapy that ensued, Chris and Jane were helped to understand that to undermine a man's job is to challenge his position in society, and that this is so threatening that he cannot help but lash out. Although at first she was reluctant to accept it, Jane came to realize that in the interest of the mental health of them both and of their two children she would have to give up her ideas of keeping up with her relatives. She could be proud of Chris and of what he had achieved, thus supporting his feeling of status instead of destroying it.

Wherever we look, we can find equally telling examples of indirect or disguised competition. In a small community where everyone attends church, traditionally each man, woman, and child puts on his best clothes, cleans himself, and presents his "Sunday best" appearance. If a child asks why he has to wash behind his ears especially thoroughly on Sunday, he will be told that he must be clean to go to the house of God. But this is the cover story. Underneath it lies social competition in its purest form. Each father is demonstrating to other fathers that he provides his family with the means to stay clean and healthy and to buy new clothes. Each mother is showing other mothers that her children are well cared for, well brought up, and that she and her husband maintain a proper household.

Such contests are engaged in so automatically that we are hardly aware of them, just as we are hardly aware of swinging our arms as we walk. But who greets whom first, who initiates and who follows, and how people acknowledge leadership are actually arenas for skirmishes every minute of our lives.

5

Contests for Dominance at Various Stages of Life

The Infant v. the Parent

The contest for dominance begins very early, when the infant learns that if he screams long enough and loud enough he can get the adults in his vicinity (usually his parents) to do more or less what he wants.

The mother on the one hand wants to make the infant comfortable and happy, and on the other wishes to impose certain rules that are the preliminaries of his training as a social creature. She also has to balance the infant's needs (for food or attention) and her own (for other duties or rest). In the face of a parent's ambivalence an infant often senses its advantage and soon comes to dominate the household. In fact, the child takes its first step in gaining status and senses the gratifications of power even before it can put into words (or thoughts) what it has achieved.

Many of the attitudes we hold and much of our behavior later in life stem from this early contest. Concrete facts may suggest that the mother is the stronger: her physical and mental capacities are superior to those of the infant. But the elements in this duel are not all concrete. The mother is conditioned by hormones, training, and social pressures not to exercise the power of which she is capable. In practice she relinquishes her status and becomes a servant to the child.

That the mother is able to do this is an evolutionary development,

33

and one of the factors that has preserved our species. Most mammals show a similar tendency, but in none is it so marked as in man. So deeply ingrained is this propensity for the child to demand attention and the mother to give it that it influences our ideals long after we grow to adulthood. Such ideas as the meek shall inherit the earth, it is the duty of the strong to protect the weak, do unto others as you would have them do unto you, and many others, all have their origin in this early experience.

That such ideas arise is what we call a cultural development, but in our species cultural influences take their place with natural phenomena as a part of our environment, and they modify our evolutionary development similarly. The bodies and behavior patterns of other species change by infinitesimal steps over great spans of time in adaptation to their environment (the type of food available, the presence or absence of predators, the type of habitat and its predominating colors, weather conditions, and a host of other factors). These changes are brought about by selection among the variations naturally occurring in the genes. In our species, changes have been brought about by the transmission from generation to generation of another kind of information: knowledge preserved in language. This transmission of information permits change to occur at an exponentially speeded rate. Thus in man changes due to cultural influences have come to outweigh the very gradual changes caused by other environmental pressures.

By this route the idea that it is right to protect the weak and helpless child, deriving from our long experience at this stage, tends to make our lives more and more child-centered, and ourselves more childlike. If we substitute the words, "the weak," "the underprivileged," "the sick and suffering," for the word "child" in the previous sentence, we have a close description of the attitudes of the modern liberal. And this attitude forms the basis of the divergence between men's societies, which usually protect their weak, and those of other animals, which eliminate them.

The Child v. the Child

The child's struggle for rank among other children is so generally recognized that the expression *sibling rivalry* has become a cliché. The most elementary rank ordering is according to age, but often other factors enter the picture. The chief modifier is our sense of "justice": that propensity to protect the weak that we have just discussed.

In an animal group the young of the same generation are constantly maneuvering from the time they are born, so that by the time they reach maturity their ranking order is pretty well established. There are, of course, the final struggles between the strongest for ultimate dominance and eventually challenges by new generations. This is the stuff out of which social order is produced.

Among birds the first-hatched chick usually has an advantage over its nestmates. It will often attempt to destroy the younger ones, either by pecking at them while they are emerging from their shells or, not even waiting for that, by tipping the other eggs out of the nest. When a natural group of birds is underpopulated the parents will protect the later-hatched and smaller chicks, but when there is overpopulation they do not interfere. Some species, like penguins, lay their eggs at intervals of a day or so, and the dominance of the firstborn by reason of its greater size then facilitates the control of their population's numbers.

Rivalries between children of the same family and between contemporaries in school and at play reflect these natural mechanisms. If they are left to their own devices, a ranking order emerges among them and is a factor in the social equilibrium they establish. However, this ranking order is seldom allowed to establish itself naturally. Younger or smaller children may claim a parent's attention because of illness, or precisely because of their relative weakness; parents may disturb the natural order in the interests of what they consider to be "justice" or "harmony."

Rank in School

Striving for status is innate. In children it takes several forms, developing from competition for the love and attention of their parents (which is biologically rooted, since the attention of the parent means sustenance and often life itself) to competition for leadership and the respect of contemporaries (which is also biologically rooted, since it leads to social order). Schools provide an arena and a training place for all kinds of struggles for status. A child can gain status by working hard, obtaining good marks and a high rank in the scholastic order. This gives him or her good standing with parents and teachers. Dominance may also be gained by excelling in sports; this usually commands the respect of contemporaries. For children who do not excel in either of these categories, musical ability or skill in painting, chess, or mechanics may bring prestige. Others gratify their strivings for standing by displays of daring. A more subtle rank definition is sometimes held by children who either cannot or will not compete in conventional areas and who establish admiring followings by being "naughty."

But in spite of all the opportunities for acquiring status by leadership or performance, it remains true that most children, like most other young animals, do not become leaders. They are followers, and perfectly happy in that role. They recognize and accept the leaders of their groups, attach themselves to one of them, and make whatever gestures of submission are called for. Problems arise for these children only when ambitious parents urge them to strive for objectives they are unable to achieve. The child who is a happy member of a group and a follower of its leaders may satisfy its need for status in other areas—say at home vis-à-vis younger brothers or sisters, or other family members. Alternatively, the child may find status in its very membership in the group, valuing his or her school, or team, or club as more prestigious than others. Although, from the outside, it may look as though a particular child holds minor standing in his social group, or is a mere hanger-on, the child himself may feel a sense of importance by identifying with the group leader or with what the group stands for. The member, or follower, feels his rank debased only if he is ousted from his group or his position diminished within it.

Prestige cannot be measured objectively or felt from the outside. We may feel that our system or group or kind of people is superior to that of others, but those others may have the same superior feelings toward us. A child who seems by outside standards to be on the lowest rung, say a juvenile delinquent, may find his status needs filled by the respect he commands in the hierarchy of a street gang, or even by membership in it. This applies, of course, not only to children but to people of every age. Whatever bestows a feeling of standing, any diminution of it is felt as pain. A child demoted from active player to standby status in his team feels annihilated, while another may be overjoyed to achieve standby status if he was not previously a member of the team at all.

Rank in Adult Life

Childhood status rivalries lay the groundwork for struggles for rank between man and man, woman and woman, man and woman, in every sphere of their lives. Not the least of these struggles are sexual relationships, where a feeling of success or failure is pivotal.

The struggle for status is easily observed in public life, whether in politics, business, the professions, or other areas where goals are clearly defined and upward or downward movement obvious. Status struggles are less easily observed on the social level, because there standards are more diffuse: the largest house, the best clothes, the most money, the finest lineage, the best job, the greatest intelligence, or any combination of these and many other values may form the criteria in different social circles. But the members of those social circles are very much aware who are their leaders, who the runners-up for leadership, who make up the rank and file, and who are the rejects of their group.

Status or status seeking between individuals is the hardest to see, partly because there are very few objective standards. Wealth, social standing, and personal attributes may play a part, but intangibles like character, leadership, and charisma also influence the standings of men and women relative to each other.

By some process of osmosis, status communicates itself. There is usually no question of assertion; status simply oozes from the holder and is perceived by his companions. Indeed, in another primate species, the Indian langur, the dominant male takes less action than subordinate ones in minor disputes, and he is quite subtle about displaying his rank. With him it is a matter of the duration of eye engagement (not unlike a dominant human's ability to stare another down), of certain grimaces, grunting, coughing, barking, and slight shifts in posture. The holding of rank in all species often includes a willingness to take responsibility, an ability to exert authority, and sometimes a preparedness to help and give protection: even the most ruthless human despot protects his own.

The follower's ability to satisfy his status needs by identification with a group goes beyond cultural influences; it is actually based on the indissoluble bond of individual to group that we find in many species. Indeed, the separation of breeding groups is so important to the lives of species that in many (to give but one example, ants), specialized odors have evolved to aid the individual to identify the members of its own group from those of an alien population, even of the same species.

Human beings sometimes make the same distinction by the same means. There are white people who aver that blacks have a peculiar odor. Some blacks of Africa contend that whites smell like corpses. Some Chinese find the odor of Caucasians offensive. Perhaps these sentiments do not reflect prejudice; there may be vestiges of odors peculiar to certain racial groups of man analogous to the distinctive odors of separate populations of ants, and some human beings may still be sensitive to them.

So strongly can an individual identify with his social group that, say, a civil servant of the lowest rank may feel superior to any person who needs his services because he identifies with the power structure of the country that employs him. He may behave very arrogantly toward a person who by any objective standard would be his superior but who needs, perhaps, a form to apply for a license or information about which department handles his particular problem.

A conspicuous example of how identification with a group can lift a person out of his own background can be found in the early days of Idi Amin of Uganda. Beginning his working life as a bellboy at the Imperial Hotel in Kampala, Amin later joined the Fourth Battalion, Kings African Rifles. Those who knew him at the time report that "within seven years he was promoted to lance-corporal and was displaying the qualities that so endeared him to his British superiors—instant obedience, fierce regimental pride, reverence toward Britain, a uniform which crackled with razor-sharp starched creases and boots with toe-caps like black mirrors." At that stage in his career he plainly identified strongly with the British ruling caste in Uganda, and this probably spurred him on his road to the presidency.

Identification with an abstract principle can also endow an otherwise humble person with a sense of status. A policeman, aware that he represents The Law, has status in his dealings with a traffic law violator, no matter how elevated the position of the latter. A highly placed member of the community stopped for speeding may find himself pleading and thus effecting a reversal of rank between them.

Such feelings about status—diverse, diffuse, and intangible as many of them are—are the elements of a very powerful force. They are part of a person's feeling about himself or herself, and eventually they affect the person's sexual drive and ability to form satisfactory intersexual relationships.

6

The Universality of the Struggle for Status

When sexual reproduction arose in the course of evolution and replaced the splitting of single cells as the chief means of perpetuating life, some kind of social ordering had to arise. If two organisms must meet and merge their genetic material in order for their kind to persist, then there must be some framework within which this is possible.

At first the sexual merging of primitive organisms may have been a random occurrence. But the very nature of the sexual process produces sufficient variations in the offspring of each generation for some to have some slight advantage over the others. This sounds so self-evident that it is hard to realize how crucial it is to the evolutionary process. In a scheme of life where the better adapted of successive generations have an edge in their ability to survive, refinements of the forms and functions of the species as a whole become inevitable. That each generation, whether of oak trees, salmon, or rabbits, produces more offspring than its habitat can support enforces a sieve action through which the best adapted, along with the lucky few, pass and carry their genes to the future, while the genes of the rest are eliminated from influencing the development of the race.

To put this in another way, imagine that a thousand people are cast adrift and that the only land in sight is an island that can accommodate not more than three hundred. The fastest swimmers, along with the lucky individuals who happen to be nearest to the island, will reach land and live to produce another generation. Suppose then that the island's resources are depleted, and this surviving group must swim to another island. In the space of comparatively few generations, the descendants of the original population will be those genetically endowed with an apparatus that permits them to have a good capacity for swimming. In this way, the sieve action automatically produces a group of people who do not look unlike their forerunners, but if you could throw both generations into the water together you would see the difference. That is not to say that the descendants would be born able to swim; they would have to be taught just as their ancestors were. But they would learn more readily and perform more skillfully because their lungs, limbs, and powers of coordination would have been inherited from parents who survived because they possessed those attributes.

It stands to reason that in a mass of primitive organisms meeting and mating randomly, the descendants of some few would, in the course of generations, develop ways of performing this function more efficiently than the rest. In the long run, these are going to become the majority and eventually supersede the less efficient. One of the ways in which some species can have an advantage over others is by adjusting their numbers to their environment's ability to sustain them. This involves the development of responses that lead to a spacing out of individuals so that there is enough food for all, and then, when the groups themselves become crowded, they, too, must be dispersed. The ways that promote this become the sources of social order.

Only recently have studies made us aware of the existence of social order in other species. Our forebears, believing that social order is a product of intelligent choice, did not believe the rest of the animal world capable of it. Taking man as the measure of all things, they were unable to detect anything that looked like their own social order in other animal groups and therefore did not recognize any. Now, as we are beginning to free ourselves of the bias of the past and can identify ourselves as part of the animal kingdom, we are able to discern the natural order of living groups and realize that order exists with no necessity for intelligence of our type.

Whenever two or more individuals of any species come together, of necessity some sort of social order ensues. When a piece of food or a place suitable for a nest or a lair is available, one individual is going to get it and the other, or others, lose it. By this very fact a certain order of precedence is set up. Moreover, besides the mechanisms that cause animals to struggle for dominance and its privileges, there must also be mechanisms that regulate the acceptance of defeat. The situation would be totally impossible if no animal were ever to give up. Perpetual fights or fights to the death over every necessity would soon eliminate any population that indulged in such uncontrolled behavior. Therefore it is not surprising that in all existing higher animals some form of social order can be found, and the propensity to act in accordance with the social habits of the group is ingrained.

All kinds of different forms of social organization exist in the animal world. Among many mammals and most birds, we recognize family groupings similar to ours. Others live in herds or flocks with an internal order of their own. Some fishes pair off for a breeding season, but otherwise are subject only to the natural laws of their groups. Even among seemingly solitary creatures, the necessities of procreation enforce some kind of social behavior at least some times of the year. Thus sexual reproduction demands the organization of creatures into breeding groups in which it is possible for the respective sexes to meet, mate, produce offspring, and provide for the nurture of the young, in a way that ensures the viability of the species.

The earth's supply of food and space is limited to a small band around its surface. It is only quite recently that the finite nature of this biosphere has come to man's attention, but nature's processes have adjusted life to this essential limitation from the time the first living thing took shape in the primordial ocean. The remarkable fact has become apparent that, barring cataclysmic events or artificial disturbance of their natural balance, animal populations never starve.

How is this possible? How can animals "know" when their numbers are too great, too few, or just right to take full advantage of available resources? The fact is that purely mechanical means adjust living matter to its sources of sustenance. If a population of bacteria increases beyond the ability of its host to sustain it, it must either find its way to a new host or perish. A barnacle larva fixes itself to a host or fails to do so in direct response to the number of other barnacle larvae already attached. When the number already fixed exceeds a certain density, an inhibition becomes operative and prevents others from joining them in that place. This simple principle applies to all living creatures: the only populations that have, or could have, survived are those that have developed ways of balancing their numbers with the capacity of their environment. In higher animals this has resulted in self-regulatory behavior that is responsible for the dispersal of animal populations over areas suitable to sustain them. Some kind of social order exists among all creatures, and each type is governed by its own conventions. There is no other way for living creatures to survive.

When we talk about the conventions of an animal group we mean those symbols that the members of the group respond to as though they were the actuality represented by the symbol. The black-headed gull "knows" by the dark feathers on the heads of its mature fellows that they are physically ready for breeding, and its behavior toward these individuals is then appropriate. The fact that each animal recognizes the conventions of its own group and responds to them, but not to those of other groups, effectively separates animals into breeding populations. (The different human languages, among other things, have much the same effect, since it is more usual to marry a person who speaks the same language than one who speaks an alien tongue.)

What is the advantage of separating animal groups into breeding populations? Here again the answer is simple, but the effect is far-reaching. When a favorable variation (a color, size, or shape that gives a creature some advantage in its habitat) appears in a group, that variation can spread far more rapidly through a small population than through a large one, where it would become diluted and probably lost. Small variations can spread through a group of limited size in relatively few generations, enabling animals to achieve that marvelous synchronization with their surroundings that we see everywhere in nature.

But it is not enough that animals are well adapted to their habitats. The habitat itself must be preserved if it is to support the creatures that use it. Population explosions deplete resources, and so uncontrolled reproduction is detrimental to the life of a group. The conventions of social order also play a part in this aspect of group survival, for, through conventions as well as through the automatic responses of nerves and glands to crowding, a group has a means of controlling its numbers and maintaining orderly societies. Many creatures, when their population density is too great, reduce the numbers of eggs they lay, mate less frequently, destroy surplus young by one means or another, or act in a variety of other ways to bring their populations back into balance.

Of the myriad examples that illustrate this, some of the easiest to discern are birds' choruses at dawn and dusk. Through these choruses birds get a feeling of how many or how few of their own kind inhabit a certain area, and this feeling sets in motion appropriate behavior to correct any imbalance. One might say that when birds sing in the morning they are taking a census. Low numbers prompt them to produce more eggs and to protect all their young, while high numbers promote opposite reactions.

We have used birds as an example, but other animals with other conventions also achieve a social order that tends to adapt them to their surroundings and to govern their numbers in the interest of the survival of all. In all higher animal species but our own, the mere arrival of an individual at sexual maturity is not enough to justify sexual function. Other conditions must be met before an animal's responses, governed by its customs, permit it to breed: it must demonstrate its fitness in social competition, and its mating must be in the interest of the total community. Although the sex drive is built into all species, it is only in man (that is to say, modern man, since the practices of tribal man were closer to those in the rest of nature) that the satisfaction of that drive is considered an automatic right of the individual and not subject to the interest of the population as a whole.

The drive for status has inevitably evolved as an instrument of the social control of reproduction, and the interlocking of sex and status is inseparable from the orderly processes of life. As we have pointed out, the amenities that are available and desirable for a species cannot be perpetually fought over. Such behavior would reduce a group to its single strongest member in short order. And besides, as V. C. Wynne-Edwards has pointed out, "the free contest for food—the ultimate limiting resource—must in the long run end in over-exploitation and diminishing returns." He showed that contest has to be, and is in fact, diverted. In most higher animals it has become a contest of purely symbolic or conventional objectives that only indirectly relate to food. That is to say, when a bird struts and displays his feathers to show that he is better than the next bird, this contest is concerned with his status in his group and not with food. But the winner in such a conventionalized contest is the one that gets both the food and other privileges. The loser only gets a share if there is plenty to go around. If not, he goes without.

The conventions of one population of animals have no meaning to any other; each develops its own rituals and displays, and these vary widely. But conventions that determine status and eligibility to rights are recognized by many kinds of animals. Out of this kind of contest, hierarchies or dominance patterns have developed. An animal's status in the hierarchy of its group is not only the most important thing in its life, it can mean life itself.

Let us now look at some of the fascinating ways in which animal hierarchies are established and see how these serve to regulate the ability of the species to survive.

For many species of fishes, birds, and mammals, a homesite is the symbol that confers status and privileges, and therefore possession of a homesite is fought for (in fact or by conventional means). The Australian bowerbirds have developed a remarkable refinement of this tendency.

The male bird constructs a bower of sticks and other vegetation on the ground. Adjoining it he builds a display stage and often decorates it with flowers, bones, and colored objects of many kinds. He may pave his bower with colored mosses, pretty pebbles, snail shells, beetle wings, parrot feathers, colored seeds, or even the yellowed skulls of small bats. He may tapestry the walls with blades of grass or leaves. If he lives near areas populated by man, he may also use fragments of glass or paper or any other attractive scrap that catches his eye.

Even more impressive, the Atlas bowerbird (and two other species) actually paint the walls of their bowers. They take bits of bark or leaves, dip them into the blue or dark green saliva they secrete, and then use these tools as we would use paintbrushes. Sometimes a bird will favor a particular color, and all his ornaments, whether flowers or berries or bits of feather or glass, will be, say, blue.

Far from displaying what some think of as "instinctive" behavior, the males perform these tasks with a great deal of deliberation and selectiveness. They spend months on the job, sometimes changing their ornaments almost every day. It would seem that they experiment with different decorative schemes until the general effect pleases them. A. J. Marshall wrote of the bowers that they are highly individual: "A glance at any bower and its decorations will reveal instantly the identity of the builder."

The fruition of this artistic endeavor comes in the courtship season when, from these beautifully constructed display stages, the males show themselves to the female who presents herself to them. Then, ensconced in their bowers, displaying both themselves and their private wealth, they compete for the privilege of mating with her. Their invitation is issued by whistling, loud calls, and spirited dance steps, and sometimes by offering a flower or some other pretty item from their collections. The females are sexually stimulated by the sight of the structures and the precious things they contain.

On the whole, the number of bowers in a given area is limited by custom. It is not the automatic right of a mature male bird to build one; he has to win this right, just as a medieval knight had to prove himself before he could become lord of the manor. According to his species the bird may build his bower afresh each year or add to it, in which case it eventually becomes a very considerable edifice. The male birds who lose the original contest spend their lives on the sidelines, awaiting a chance to take over one of the sites if a reigning possessor is removed by death or injury.

The mere possession of a bower site does not allow the victorious bird to rest on his laurels. His neighbors make constant attempts at raiding his property, and he himself sallies forth in attempts to damage the bowers of others. If he can manage this, the bird with the damaged bower becomes one rival less for the attention of the female when she comes. Marshall gave a colorful description of this perpetual jousting:

> During the period of prenuptial gonad development neighboring males of the satin bower-bird are continually aware of each other's movements and raid each other's bowers and wreck and steal the coloured display-objects whenever they are left unguarded. . . . A wrecking rival will . . . hop in stealthily, rather than fly boldly through the open timber. . . . He comes by the most direct route from his position at the time he observes that the bower is undefended. At the bower the marauder works swiftly and silently and tears down beakfuls of the walls and strews them about in disorder. A wrecker rarely completes his task before he is disturbed by the swift swish of wings of the owner. Usually he snatches up a beakful of blue feathers or glass as he flies. He never stays to fight.

It struck Wynne-Edwards that this behavior was very significant in terms of adjusting the population's numbers to its habitat. He suggested that since it imposed stress on the contestants, this stress would increase when their numbers became too many and would serve "to discourage at least some attempts to establish new bowers in 'unauthorized' places, especially by individuals of inferior status."

The female bowerbird is in no way concerned with the preliminary contest of the males. However, once the males have determined among themselves which are fit to possess bowers, the female ready for mating will come to the bowers and present herself to one of the males. The bower is not the nesting site. The impregnated female goes off, builds her own nest, and raises her family in seclusion. The bower is nothing less than a "cultural" symbol demonstrating the status of the male among his peers. Presumably the higher his status the more eligible he is—and the more females he gets a chance to impregnate.

Much like man, the bowerbird does not depend on an anatomical feature (such as plumage, crest, mane, or colorful markings) to display his rank, but uses artifacts. In fact, the most gifted architects and interior decorators among them (particularly the Maypole builders, the avenue builders and the tepee builders) are the least impressive in their physical appearance. They are crestless and virtually indistinguishable from the females.

As in human pageantry and tradition, the bowerbird displays some colorful practices. If we look beyond them, we discover their significance. The restriction of the number of bower sites limits the number of males available for breeding (since the females only present themselves to possessors of bowers). The limitation of the number of breeding males controls the number of offspring produced, which regulates the number of the next generation and keeps it in consonance with the resources of the area.

Another staunch property owner and inveterate fighter is the fiddler crab. Many naturalists have been intrigued by its habits, and among them A. S. Pearse gave us a vivid picture:

Each individual jealously guards the area about his own burrow, and immediately attacks any invader of this territory. His pugnacity is ever ready to show itself against his fellows that swarm about him and against numerous competitors of other kinds that also seek to eke out an existence from the area he has chosen for his own. . . . In fighting males face each other, and often dance about excitedly, at the same time frantically waving the small chela. The large chelae are locked together, like two men shaking hands, and each contestant attempts to break off his opponent's claw by a sudden wrench. The strain is so great that when one of the fighters loosens his hold rather than lose his claw, he is often thrown backward into the air, sometimes as much as a meter.

R. W. G. Hingston believed that the oversized claw "is a psychological weapon, and for this reason [is] brilliantly colored, being a shining pink or bright crimson that glitters when brandished, like a fiery torch."

It is clear that the magnificent claw, cumbersome as it may be, enables its owner to assert his status in his community. Here we see again the close connection between an animal's defense of his territory by fighting others of the same sex and his social acceptance as a breeder. The extent of the territory limits the number of winners. The limitation of winners controls the number of breeders and therefore of their offspring, which brings us back to the essential: enough food for all. We can see the same mechanism at work in myriad forms in species after species.

Among the shrews (*Sorex araneus*) squeaking, screaming, and posturing settle the relative social standing of the males. The fighting that precedes breeding in this species has been displaced into a symbolic contest that, in this case, is vocal. The hammerhead fruit bat also establishes status with its voice. Of all the mammals, no other can boast a comparable vocal organ, which may be as much as one third of its total body volume.

The American alligator also bellows. If this threat is not sufficient to cow his opponent into acknowledging his superiority, he fights for it. His roar proclaims his dominance and at the same time challenges all the males within earshot.

As far back as 1874 Darwin was aware (as are today's hunters) that the roar of the stag is not a call to the hinds, but that on the contrary it is the female, when the time is ripe, who calls the male. When the red deer, at home in Scotland, roar and spar and compete, sometimes rearing on their hind legs and punching at each other with their forehoofs, they do so to establish and maintain their male hierarchy.

When the sea elephant comes ashore and claims his territory for the mating season, he likewise defends it by roaring and by the intimidating effect of his massive size.

The black bear signals his superiority by rearing up as high as he can stand and gnawing the bark of trees, thus effectively marking the territory he stakes out as his own and announcing his height and might to all that might challenge him.

These are some of the ways that winners assert their status. The loser also has a vocabulary of symbolic communication. At its very simplest, the loser simply turns tail and flees. The interesting point is that the winner accepts the gesture and usually does not pursue the fleeing animal beyond a certain limit. Whatever one may call this kind of behavior, instinct or learning or a melding of the two, it is part of an animal's behavioral repertoire.

Some species turn away their heads to acknowledge defeat. To do this in the heat of contest is to suggest (in our terms) a throwing down of weapons, since the animal's most powerful ones are usually his teeth, tusks, or horns, all located on or around his head. His communication then is like our saying, "Look, I am no longer fighting you. I have withdrawn my weapons."

Among the many different signals that are used by various species, but carry similar meaning, some are far more complex. Many wild canines roll over on their backs in imitation of a pup when their reflexes inform them that they are beaten. This signal approaches language in its abstraction. To translate it we would have to say, "I am toward you as the puppy is. I am no longer hostile to you. Act toward me as you would to a puppy, who cannot challenge you." Obviously, the animal cannot and does not think in these terms, but it does react to the gesture as we would react to these words.

In other species, notably in some primates, the vocabulary of the loser borrows signals of sexual communication and uses them symbolically. A baboon female, for instance, when ready for mating, presents her rump to the chosen male. Since there is no contest between male and female, any more than there is between adult and cub, this gesture can also be used by a loser to denote, "I am no longer challenging you." If we make an analogy between this kind of communication and language, it is comparable to the use of a word or phrase in a different context changing its meaning—that is, a metaphor. Students of animal behavior have frequently misread the female's sexual invitation as a "submission" to the male, but it cannot be that, since there is no contest between them. But when the male uses the same gesture to another male, or a female to another female, they are conveying the metaphor "regard me as you would a female who is inviting a male to intercourse," which must remove hostility. Conversely, when a female primate mounts another female the action is not sexual, but the metaphorical use of the gesture that indicates the male's role.

In human nonverbal communication we make use of similar metaphorical gestures. A man who raises his hat to denote friendliness may not know it, but he is using the gesture of the medieval knight who raised his visor to indicate that he was no longer in contest. Today we accept the raising of a hat in its current context and acknowledge its current meaning, as without doubt other animals do when they respond to a loser's signal.

What can happen to losers is demonstrated by the stickleback and the jewel fish. When a dominant stickleback drives other males away from his rather large territory, the losers fail to develop nuptial colors and also their ability to build nests. This is an equivalent of human impotence! In the case of the jewel fish, as G. K. Noble has noted, "rarely will more than one pair breed in a tank of seventy-five to one hundred gallons. The reason for this is that the breeding male and later the female are so active in defense of their territory that they keep all other sexually mature fish in a state of agitation, which prevents them from claiming any other suitable spot in the tank for egg-laying." In this, perhaps, they are not unlike a harassed human who, after the frustrations of the day, does not feel like making love by the time he (or she) gets home!

It is of great importance to social order that losers as well as winners abide by their conventions. This acceptance by both winners and losers is facilitated by neural and hormonal action, and we are aware of these forces in ourselves as well as in their more pristine state in other animals. They are at the root of those "turned on" or "turned off" feelings that we referred to in our second chapter and that, because we believe them to be so closely connected with human impotence and frigidity, deserve extensive and deeper exploration.

7

Masculine and Feminine

No matter how diverse animal societies are, no matter how varied their types of organization nor how different their anatomical structures, there is one fundamental trait that characterizes them all. It is that once a social order has been established in any group, it is adhered to. The dominant animals take on the privileges and responsibilities that are associated with dominance, and the subordinate animals accept their situation.

What leads an animal to accept submission? By our codes we believe in the philosophy Robert Bruce learned from the spider: "If at first you don't succeed, try, try, and try again." Yet in general, a failure to gain leadership has a dampening effect upon our ardor. If we have failed once we are more likely to fail again in the same endeavor than to achieve the goal, although it *is* sometimes done. For other animals it is almost impossible.

The reason for this lies in a mechanism that resides in every animal above the most primitive. The nervous system, whether it operates via a brain or a less complex ganglionic system, has two levels of operation. The simpler level facilitates an action by relaying an impulse to the necessary muscle. The more complex one sets up a mood, or a state of being, that promotes suitable action.

To give an example of this: we know that it is possible for any one of us to hit another person. We have only to will the action and the necessary muscles will clench a hand into a fist, raise an arm, and cause it to strike. But we also know that we will not do such a thing unless we are either angry or afraid of being attacked.

What in ourselves we call a mood and in other animals we may call a state of being (fear, hate, anger, love, etc.) is initiated by the nervous system but actually made effective by the hormones. We might say that in this instance the hormones act as executors of the nervous system's directives. Only when hormonal secretions have put the body into a state that the brain has perceived to be necessary can the corresponding action take place. Man alone can take action by means of will in the absence of mood, but when the mood is lacking the action cannot be as effective as when it is present. If in the course of reading such a statement you decide to strike your neighbor to prove that it is possible, undoubtedly you will find that you can do it. But if you compare the blow that you make with one that you might make as a result of a surge of anger, you will see that the first action is a pale imitation of the second. It is the surge of anger that promotes all the changes in the body that ready it for a fighting response.

Other hormones impose contrary responses, like fear, submission, or giving up. For the survival of any group of animals it is just as important for its individuals to give up when necessary as it is for them to be able to fight when necessary. Otherwise there would be nothing but fighting to the death among them, which obviously would *not* promote the survival of the species.

To understand how this mechanism works we should take a look at the hormonal mechanisms that are responsible for it. Basically, all individuals of the same species are endowed with the same type of hormonal equipment, but slight variations in quantity or, perhaps, quality spell out the differences in each generation's competition for status.

Recent research at primate centers has shown a significant correlation between the status of an individual in a group and testosterone (male hormone) production. It is difficult to determine whether enhanced hormone production leads to high status or high status to increased production of the hormone. Probably, as in most organic states, there is a circular effect in which an animal that has high status and high aggression also has high testosterone levels.

When experimenters forcibly interfered with the social standing of a dominant animal (either by physically restraining it, by removing it to another compound where it had not established status, or by other means), its testosterone level dropped. But when experimenters gave a lower-ranking animal injections of testosterone, its aggressiveness was enhanced and its social status rose. Conversely, when an experimenter manipulated a low-ranking animal into higher status (by removing from its compound those that outranked it, or by other means), its testosterone levels rose. Here we can see clearly a connection between sex hormone production and social status.

Dr. Adrian Perachio, the chief of the neurophysiological laboratory at Yerkes Regional Primate Center of Emory University in Lawrenceville, Georgia, found an aggression center in the brain that can be influenced by electrodes implanted in the hypothalamus (a part of the brain situated at its base). When he stimulated such electrodes in the brain of a normally subdominant animal he found that it would attack a dominant member of the group. Its sexual behavior was also affected, for it was able to mount a higher-ranking female than it would normally be able to approach. This again confirms the close connection between sexuality and social standing. It also seems that no animal, and no man either, is innately "top dog." The potential is present, perhaps equally, in all, and the circumstances of individual experience play a large role.

Strangely enough, the male hormone testosterone also plays a role in the determination of female sexuality and status. Our idea that there is a fundamental difference between males and females is based on our visual impression of adult forms. But recent research indicates that as one traces the development of individuals backward, there is progressively less difference between male and female. Our own eyes and experience show us that there is little difference between sexes in early childhood, and we know that at earlier fetal stages the differences are even slighter. At the very earliest stage of embryonic development we now know that all of us are in essence female. In those who are genetically destined to become male, a sequential mechanism transforms the genital buds into male organs during the first trimester; in the absence of this mechanism, the bud develops into female organs.

Because males produce more testosterone and females more estrogen, it has been assumed that sexual receptivity is determined by the predominant sex hormone, and indeed this is so in most mammals. In the case of primates, including man, however, it is not so. B. J. Everitt and his colleagues at the University of Birmingham, Alabama, discovered this surprising fact by checking the blood level of the respective hormones at stages in the sexual behavior of rhesus monkeys.

They removed the ovaries of the female monkeys by surgery, and thereby stopped the production of estrogen and progesterone, the female sex hormones. Unexpectedly, this did not diminish the female's sex drive. But the males who were paired with these altered females did not respond to them. This corresponds to the well known but insufficiently appreciated observation that the human female does not lose sexual desire following the removal of her ovaries. However, when the experimenters removed the adrenal glands of the female monkeys (which secrete a variant of male hormone called androstenedione), they found their sexual receptivity greatly reduced.

To clarify the respective roles of the male and female sex hormones, the investigators next removed the ovaries from a number of rhesus monkeys. At the same time they maintained normal hormone balance with injections of estrogen. Some animals also had their adrenal glands removed. They were then divided into three groups: the first received only estrogen; the second estrogen and androstenedione; the third received both estrogen and a second secretion of the adrenal gland, dehydroepiandrosterone. Each female was paired once a day with the same male monkey over a period of thirty days. The female control animals, with their adrenal glands intact, displayed normal sexual receptivity and initiated the majority of all the sexual contacts. The females without adrenal glands that received estrogen alone or together with the second adrenal secretion showed greatly reduced receptivity. These experiments have underlined the paradox that in primates, including man, the male hormones—secreted partly by the ovaries but mainly by the adrenal glands—promote sexual receptivity in a female. The female hormones promote her sexual attractiveness to the male: it is a stimulant that triggers the male's ability to respond. The "male" sex hormone produced by the female also has the important function of sustaining her responsiveness to the male's advances.

An intriguing sidelight is that folk wisdom seems to have had an intuitive understanding of what scientific demonstration has only now uncovered, that the presence of male sex hormone in women makes them sexually more responsive. In Mediterranean countries it is commonly believed that women who have moustaches are far more passionate than their smooth-skinned sisters. In 1857 A. A. Tardieu attested to this belief in his book *Etude Medico-Legale sur les Attentats aux Moeurs,* in which he stated that sensual women are hirsute. We now know that an increase in the function of the adrenal gland in women produces a greater quantity of male sex hormone, which, among other effects, also fosters facial hair growth.

Almost as if nature wants to make the intangibility of sexual differentiation quite clear, she provides us with an example so extreme it offers a natural equivalent of a laboratory demonstration. It is to be found in the life cycle of the little fish of the wrasse family that can be found off the shores of Australia in the waters of the Great Barrier Reef.

Dr. D. R. Robertson, a zoologist of the University of Queensland at Brisbane, observed that the removal of a male from a group of these fish (*Labroides diminatus*) has a rather startling result: the dominant female becomes a male! A few hours after the male's disappearance, the head female begins to display male behavior. She patrols the territory and aggressively courts the other females. Within four days her behavior cannot be distinguished from a male's. Within fourteen to eighteen days she becomes a functioning male, able to produce sperm.

The social regulatory functioning of status is crystal clear in this case. As Dr. Robertson wrote in his report on his more than two years' study of these fish, "probably all the females are capable of changing sex, and most (perhaps all) of them have elements of testicles within perfectly functioning ovaries."

What makes this example so interesting from our point of view is that wholesale sex transformations by the females are prevented by "a chain of authority extending downward from the lone male." In spite of having formerly been a female himself (like most other males of this species), he bullies the strongest female, who in turn bullies the female under her, and so on down the social scale. It is the factor of status, pure and simple, that determines which female will become the male and regulates the group as a whole. "As long as a wrasse remains under the stress of domination its body does not produce the hormones necessary to effect a sex change, but once the stress is removed hormone production is no longer inhibited and transformation occurs."

The process of the development of a male from a female is called *protogyny,* and it is not uncommon among tropical fish. We find many other examples in nature that the same biological equipment may go either way. Of course the nonhuman primates, being so nearly related to us, offer us analogies closer to home, and so the experiments and clinical observations just described are very upsetting to our conventional ideas about human male-female relations.

It is clear that in primates the female is meant to be the initiator and the male the responder in sexual approaches. Since the human female possesses the same hormonal arrangements as the female monkey, how is it she has abandoned her biological role as initiator? Or did she really? Even superficial observation indicates that at least on a symbolic level, she did not. While her overt gestures are usually not as explicit as the corresponding ones in the nonhuman primates, just the same she is constantly "presenting" herself symbolically, by the kind of clothes she wears and the cosmetics she uses. The male responds to these signals within the limits of cultural training. Of course in our societies the male no more considers himself invited to sexual intercourse when he meets a female wearing lipstick than does the female consider she is issuing an invitation when she applies her makeup. Nevertheless her clothing and grooming are designed to make her attractive to males in general, and males in general respond to the stimuli they see.

This connection between the male hormone and the status of both males and females provides an explanation for the vastly increased competitiveness and aggressiveness of our species. In modern man, both drives are so powerful that they can hardly be contained within the bounds of intrasex competition and species convention, as they are in other animals.

We think of carnivorous animals of all kinds as aggressive, and they have to be so in order to overcome their prey. But other carnivores do not kill unless they are in need of food; when they are satiated their aggressive drive is blunted. Their only other grounds for fighting are the establishment of rank (indirectly, to acquire a mate) or to defend a territory (which is preliminary to mating), and all this fighting is governed by rigid behavioral conventions.

Man's aggressiveness and competitiveness have the same roots but have gone beyond biological necessity. Now, just as sexuality knows no season, aggression knows no bounds. In man's supersexuality and the aggressiveness that goes with it, we may find an explanation for such human phenomena as rape, blood feuds, and fights to the death, which are almost unheard of in other species. The new knowledge that aggression and dominance and sex are so closely intertwined that each of them is in some way a reflection of the others may help us to understand man's most puzzling trait: his brutality. For, as we recognize our supersexuality, we must understand the superaggressiveness that is produced by the same hormonal configuration.

This connection clarifies many kinds of behavior. Probably most clearly, it makes apparent the reason why soldiers of victorious armies can rarely be prevented from raping the women of conquered nations. The feeling of dominance over the defeated males that comes with victory and the hormonal stimulation of the fighting are both part of the drive for sexual completion, while the sense of inferiority and submission that goes with defeat is a powerful inhibitor of sexual impulse.

This connection also provides a clue to the sexual arousal (often not recognized and usually not admitted) that many people feel in the presence of violence and may explain the otherwise incomprehensible popularity of violence as entertainment, whether in books and films or in boxing matches, bullfights, cockfights, and other blood sports.

Together with man's infantilization and his resulting ungoverned sexuality (as opposed to the mature and governed sexuality of other creatures) and with his overcrowding (which may be an aspect of infantilization), we think that this understanding of man as a supersexual and *therefore* superaggressive species offers a more solid explanation of our overall aggressiveness than any other.

Sex, however, masculine or feminine, aggressive or passive, while biologically executed by the individual, is primarily at the service of the group as a whole, as is made clear in the case of the little wrasse. As Dr. Robertson commented, "the social organization is a framework within which the selective process works," and it is this aspect that we want to examine more closely now.

8

Animal Societies and Human Groups

When it comes down to essentials, there is really little difference between the ways other animals react to each other and the ways human beings do. If we peel off the veneer of culture and look at our basic behavior impartially, it is hard to find any point where we could decisively draw a distinction. And if this thought makes any of us feel uncomfortable we should remind ourselves that any equation of man with other animals is not to the detriment of man. Although through lack of knowledge, or misunderstanding, it was not realized until recently, the behavior of other species is at least as orderly as our own, and in some respects perhaps more so. The parallels between the social behavior of other species and our own can be startling if we make the effort to compare them without prejudice or preconceived notions.

As soon as two people come together, one is going to set the pace and the other will follow. If they can't agree there will be a discussion or an argument until one or the other of them wins and thus establishes his or her rank, at least temporarily. This pattern is quite universal. Even though egalitarianism is the ideal of modern societies, it is rarely achieved. It makes no difference whether the individuals are young or old, whether the society in which they live is simple or sophisticated, which part of the world or which point in time one examines, the presence of more than one individual enforces an order of precedence. This extends into every kind and size of group from the smallest assembly of people through families and clans, clubs and organizations, cities, states, and nations. In many animal societies, although not in all, social ranking is more rigid than in our own. It seems to be easier for man to change his relative position. For example, when a general is traveling by sea there is no question but that the captain of the ship is in command; when a high-ranking person enters a doctor's office, it is the doctor who takes charge, but that person's rank is restored as soon as he leaves.

Almost all the activities that tend to order the social life of other animals also find their equivalents in man's. V. C. Wynne-Edwards has described with a mass of detail how almost all animal groups are regulated by what he calls "epideictic displays." The croaking choruses of frogs in the evenings identify a frog with his group: make him aware of the others, how many or how few there are, their location, their readiness for breeding, and any other information he needs, just as the nightly howling of wolves or the symphonies of birds do for them. Nor are vocal signals the only ones that serve to hold groups of animals together and subordinate their individual lives to their mutual advantage. Some habitually use what have been called parade grounds, where whole groups gather at certain times of day to display fine feathers or acrobatic flight, or merely make their presence known to their kind at watering holes or salt licks.

In man's societies until our own times, the function served by these gatherings of animals was largely effected by religious rites and local ceremonies. In the days when every person in a small town attended church on Sundays or brought his produce to a weekly market or joined the dances on the village green on May Day, each person became aware of his neighbor, whether he was in good health or ill, whether his farm or business was prospering, whether his sons or daughters had reached marriageable age. All this served to identify him with his group and make him a part of it. Moreover, the fact that such gatherings made a person feel a part of a community also made that person responsive to social pressures in a very similar way that an animal responds to the pressure of numbers or other group influences.

As we are writing these words, sitting on a balcony in Marrakech in Morocco, a great clanging and banging of instruments draws our attention to a procession in the street below. Almost any day such a procession can be seen somewhere in this city, sometimes with as few as a dozen participants and sometimes thirty or forty strong. The women are dressed in the loveliest of their colorful gowns and finery, the men in their hooded djellabas, and their musical instruments draw all eyes to their presence. The last members of the procession drag an open cart carrying a slaughtered sheep, a crate containing a dozen bottles of oil, one or more large sacks, and similar objects.

This ceremony is a part of the formalities of a marriage. A bridegroom and his family are conveying these objects as gifts to his bride's family, and for us the most interesting aspect of the procession is that it takes the most circuitous route possible, so that all the town can see the gifts. The implications of this custom are in no way different from the necessity among territorial animals for the male to possess a homesite before he can breed. It shows that the bridegroom is a man of substance, that he has the means to support a family. The community at large is offered proof of this, so that it may make its own judgment and thereby establish his status.

Today in industrialized countries our lives are no longer—or to a much less degree—influenced by church attendance or local ceremonies, but we are still subject to public opinion, as is shown by the fact that in many ways we behave differently in public from the way we act in private. Nor would it press the analogy too far to note the human displays of fine feathers at such conventional parade grounds as resorts and night clubs; our acknowledgment of the external symbols of rank like fine clothes, educated speech, an expensive car, knowledge of the arts; the reverence we give to outstanding athletic performance and to beauty of face or figure. As in other animals, in each of our social groups different conventions hold sway, but their effect is the same. They sort out dominant from follower, winner from loser.

In modern societies the pressure of public opinion no longer affects our breeding habits—at least, not consciously. (It is well within the bounds of possibility, however, that overcrowding may affect us *un*consciously much as it affects other animals: that is, by reducing the inclination of many to breed at all, by increasing sexual deviance, by inducing more stillborn offspring, and so on.)

The forces of social pressure, which have played such important parts in the molding of our species, may be attenuated or vestigial in us, but they are still present and in many ways influence what we do and think, even when we believe that we are acting as free agents. We feel conscious of an ability to make choices, and this makes us believe that to some extent we guide our own fate. Any suggestion that the private options we exercise are also influenced by social forces largely outside our control would meet with heated objection.

If we were to ask a person why he puts on his most becoming clothes to go to church, to a meeting, or to a club, he might reply, "Well, when I know I'm going to meet a lot of people I like to look my best." Another might say, "Oh, I like to get dressed up a bit sometimes. It makes me feel good." Any idea that their "dressing up" is similar to the social competition that takes place in other animal species would strike them as incongruous. Yet they are motivated by the same force that causes a bird to display his fine feathers or a deer to joust with his antlers: an urge to impress others with the symbols of one's social status.

There are many such forces working in us behind the scenes, so to speak. They are so automatic that they never impinge on our thoughts, but they are built in to our very being, are part of our most elementary responses, not because it is either "good" or "bad," but simply because this is the way living things have developed.

Under the impact of technological culture and medical advances that preserve winner and loser alike, these forces of social order (conventional competition, leading to social ranking, leading to special privileges including preferential breeding rights) *may* be less decisive in man than in other species, but they may not. In any case we still retain the mechanisms, and our bodies still respond (via the brain's interpretation) to their stimuli.

So far in this book we have shown that some of our systems of organizing groups and group hierarchies are very similar to those of other species, and that we have certain similar behavioral characteristics, especially those concerned with status and sex. We too have pecking orders and methods of achieving rank; we too have social and symbolic methods of showing domination; we too feel most reassured when our place in the group is clear and accepted.

But we also have to face problems that other animals seldom encounter: not only do we have to rank ourselves in a male or female pecking order according to our own sex, but we must also find a place in intersexual hierarchies at home and at work.

We also have one or two other traits that other animals do not have but that create problems for us. We are hypersexual all the year round. We are also very aggressive, and we have the longest dependent childhood, both absolutely and relatively, of any animal species.

During this dependency period we learn to equate feelings of dependence with love and also to look after those who are helpless. This later on encourages us to care for all who are weak, enabling them to survive and breed and bear offspring that become problems in their turn.

Up to now we have dealt mainly with our similarities to the rest of the animal kingdom. Now we shall look more closely at our differences, the problems they bring, and possible solutions.

9

Intersex Competition
in Man

So far we have been discussing how competition within species, whether overt or symbolic, serves to retain the best-adapted individuals and promotes social order and evolutionary changes and advances. We have not dwelt upon the fact that conventional competition is confined within the bounds of each sex, male pitted against male and female against female. Of course, in some animal species the dominance factor is more marked than in others, and in many it does not fall into a direct hierarchical pyramid. Still, dominance exists to some degree in all higher animals. But until we come to modern man there is no such thing as competition for status between male and female, and for a very good reason.

To take a simple illustration, we can see that it is perfectly possible to arrange a competition among tenors or among silversmiths, to find who is the best tenor or who the most gifted worker in silver. We cannot imagine organizing a contest in which tenors and silversmiths compete with each other, for what could such a competition decide? The best ... what? The best man? Hardly, for who can compare a well-produced high C and a well-made gadroon border, or the relative survival value to his population of the genes of the man who possesses these skills?

In all other animal groups, the roles of the sexes are completely separate and distinct, and therefore separate and distinct attributes are needed by each. No useful purpose could be achieved by competition *between* the sexes, and so it simply does not happen. In man, and especially in modern man, it does. If male-female bonding developed for the protection of the young, as we believe it did, then why is it that so much marital strife exists in man?

All kinds of explanations could be offered to account for this. Some would assert that cultural patterns, carried through generations by example and training, are responsible. These would include egalitarian ideals that attempt to blur differences of sex, race, age, or degree of skill and assert that each individual must be judged in his or her own terms and not in comparison with others. One could make a case that man's supersexuality and its concomitant superaggressiveness have spilled over the borderlines of brotherly and sisterly rivalry into a general rivalry that knows no boundary of sex. One could also say that since our culture is no longer so dependent on a separation of roles between the sexes, and this separation of roles is increasingly fading, it is not surprising that contests for status should also become less sex-confined.

Any, or all, of these points may be factors. But do they tell the whole story? It seems to us that in many ways they are results, the froth on the top of the coffee. They tell us nothing about the planting of the tree, the ripening of the bean, the drying and selecting and grinding of it—all the processes that must be completed before that froth can show itself on the top of the steaming liquid.

By now it is fairly well established that of the two sexes, in Homo sapiens, the female is biologically the stronger. Statistics show that the survival rate of female infants in the first year of life is rather higher than that for the male, indicating that the male is more fragile. Females also tend to live slightly longer than males. Although this is sometimes accounted for as being due to their less hazardous occupations, this explanation does not really hold water since, at least until the present century, few occupations equaled childbirth in risk to life.

That the female should be strong and resilient is really quite natural, for the immense stresses to which her body and emotions are subjected in childbirth must have ensured such an evolutionary development. How, then, has it come about that we all think of the male as the stronger sex? To answer this question, we must examine the time when our precursors became hunters rather than gatherers.

Of itself hunting is neither a specifically male nor a specifically female occupation. It is undertaken in some species by one and in others by the opposite sex. For instance, among lions and hyenas the females hunt and provide meat. In the case of man, the long and complete helplessness of infancy precludes this. The female, bound by her biological role to remain with her young, could not go hunting or remain away from her home base for any length of time. Thus the hunting role devolved upon the male. And so it has come about that in our species all the physical attributes that contribute to hunting skills (longer legs, stronger muscles) have been selected and preserved in the males, and to this extent they are indeed physically stronger, although not biologically so. In terms of survival, it is the female who has the edge.

In view of this it seems rather strange, at first, that the role of the male has traditionally been the more esteemed, and usually (although not always) the male has played the dominant social role. But if we consider all the ingredients that go into making this particular cup of coffee we can identify several possible explanations.

At the level of the froth on the top, two considerations are readily apparent. The first is unquestionably the larger size and greater muscular strength of the male. Greater size is a decisive factor in dominance throughout nature. The second is the glamour attached to the hunting role—a glamour associated with danger encountered, trials of strength and spirit, knowledge and skillful preparations. One might counter this with the observation that gathering food and preparing it, bearing and raising children, also demanded knowledge, skills, and the ability to endure danger. But the day-to-day events of life become less valued by their familiarity. The hunt was a special occasion no matter how frequently it occurred. It involved rites to propitiate the spirits of the hunted animal; the trophy provided a feast and a grounds for celebration, an occasion that for us might be equated with a banquet after a long period of home cooking.

In addition, the superior size and muscular strength the male developed in his selection for hunting naturally conferred on him the role of protector of the family and group. A protector automatically assumes leadership.

When man's societies became agricultural there was a slight decline in the degree of male dominance, as is indicated by the fact that goddesses personifying fertility became objects of worship for many peoples. Nevertheless, the male's role as warrior and defender continued and to a large extent preserved his position of social dominance. But as our species moved gradually toward industrialization and urbanization, and the hunting of food became the symbolic amassing of money, some of the heroic aspects of the male's function began to fade.

Today, in the absence of a hunting economy, the things that a man can do and a woman cannot or that a woman can and a man cannot are reduced to insemination and childbirth. With all the prepackaged foods, laundry machines, and other labor-saving devices available, a man can take care of a house or a child if he has to. Similarly, a woman can operate in a man's field as well as he can. Therefore the road is open to indiscriminate competition between male and female for the same goals. We are no longer confined to contests between male and male or female and female to sort out the best equipped of each.

These explanations would appear to account for the traditional prestige of the male role in human societies, and they give a clue as to why the female, now largely freed from her traditional occupations, should seek to identify herself with it. Still, it is hard to understand the enormous resistance and antagonism the female's redefinition of roles arouses in the majority of males. The sustained attempt to "keep woman in her place," the denigration of the value of her labor, the last-ditch efforts to deny her entry into jobs she is perfectly capable of performing, the ridiculing of her efforts to find rewarding occupation outside the home, the forms of contempt by joke and "put-down" that are inflicted upon women who excel—all must have deep-seated causes.

In looking for these causes we find ourselves at the core of the conflict between the sexes.

It is far more difficult for a male to establish his identity than for a female to establish hers. In the early years of our lives we are all subject to our mothers; our fathers are more distant figures. When childhood comes to an end and adolescence arrives, it is far easier for a girl to take on the role of a woman than for a boy to become a man. The girl has only to continue to identify with her mother, learn her skills, and observe her as a model for behavior. But the adolescent boy must break away from his mother and become something else. His manhood is therefore more vulnerable than his sister's womanhood. Margaret Mead has suggested that the secret and often drastic initiation rites of the boy into manhood in some tribal societies represent a symbolical annulment of his life until then and his rebirth as a man.

As a young adult the male must then prove himself again and again. When new ties of affection bind him again to a woman in courtship and marriage, he must constantly be on his guard to preserve his male identity. Consider the deep shame of a young man who is called a "mama's boy" or an older man who is considered henpecked. Submission to a female is associated in his feelings with childhood; to be a man, he must be free of woman and assert himself over her. He probably fears that any submission to a female in *any* area would cause him to slip a notch or two in the esteem of other males; therefore his need to appear dominant over females is a part of his feeling about his own rank among his fellow males.

The young male's favorite pastime of bragging to his friends about his conquests of females reveals much about man's central dilemma: the complications conferred by his long childhood. A male asserting his superiority over other males by showing off his muscular strength (for example in games on beaches) is an equivalent of the displays of strength, agility, and male beauty that are normally found in the rest of the animal world. But when the male asserts his male superiority at the expense of the female, we have a manifestation that is peculiarly human.

Whatever the reasons for the greater value put upon the male role, it is a fact of life in a majority of human societies. However, cultural acceptance of the male "dominant" role does not always reflect the facts.

In nearly all families in our Western orbit, whether they are of Anglo-Saxon, Teutonic, Slavic, or Latin cultures, and whatever the degree of "ceremonial" male dominance, it is apparent that the woman usually runs the home. From the time a girl is a tiny child, her chief experience of dominance is of her mother running the household. From the time she gets up in the morning until the time she goes to bed at night, the traditional housewife is running things. Whether her household is a large one including servants or dependent relatives, or a smaller one with only her immediate family, she directs its maintenance. She supervises the activities of those who help her; she orders the supplies she needs; she instructs her children. The traditional housewife has no choice but to be dominant; dominance is thrust upon her, expected of her.

The arrival of the husband home at the end of his day's work presents a problem about the distribution of power. This problem is solved differently in different cultures, and even within cultures there is a good deal of variation in the ways individuals deal with it. The most usual solution is that on the whole the man accepts the woman's dominance in the arena of their domestic lives (even if there is a pretense that it is otherwise), and she accepts his outside of it. The woman is usually dominant in the home even in cultures that appear to be totally male oriented: where *machismo* is cultivated, for instance, or in the extremely patriarchal culture of the Jews, where the woman's importance in the home is ritualized in the ceremonies she performs and the prayers it is her duty to say.

In this kind of situation there are obviously many areas of overlapping authority, and unless behavior follows certain ground rules they become the bases of dissension and strife. Peaceful solutions call for considerable diplomacy on the part of the woman. Typical is the attitude of the Latin wife who will defer to her husband in form and words but run things as she wishes just the same. Her position is like that of the prime minister in a monarchy: the king or queen holds the ceremonial power, but it is the prime minister who makes the decisions. His formula is to convey suggestions to the monarch in such a way that the monarch believes they emanate from himself. He will also present these ideas in public as though they indeed originated with the monarch. The Latin woman will tell her children, "Your father says. . . ." or "Your father wants. . . ." while in fact guiding them the way she wishes them to go. She will also maintain in public that any event in her household—the redecoration of a room, a decision to take a vacation or to buy a country property—takes place at her husband's wish, whereas often the guiding idea is her own. Her tact pleases the man, for all he really wants is an acknowledgment of his ceremonial rank in the household. If he were given the actual job of supervising all the details of running it, he would immediately abdicate.

At the other extreme, there is a tendency in the modern Anglo-Saxon family for the woman to expect public acknowledgment as an equal partner in its affairs. Paradoxically, in desiring (and to a large extent having) a partnership with her husband in the running of their home, the Anglo-Saxon wife wields less authority than the Latin woman who accepts the prime-minister role. As a partner the Anglo-Saxon woman shares power equally with her husband, while the Latin woman as a prime minister actually has complete control.

Camouflaged or overt, total or shared, the dominant status of the female in the domestic life of man is a practical outcome of the change from a hunting to an agricultural economy and eventually to an urban one. Moreover, within the span of this century, when increased mobility has tended to loosen family bonds and fewer individuals live together to share domestic labors, the female has had to take over more and more duties—so many, in fact, that without the assistance of labor-saving devices it would hardly be possible for her to accomplish them. As a result, she has become largely an administrator of her home, a role that is difficult to distinguish in any fundamental way from her husband's administration of his work. It is not surprising that a wife is unwilling to acknowledge her role as subordinate or cater to her husband's need for recognition. As a result we have a state of affairs similar to a country divided into two equally matched kingdoms in which there are constant maneuverings to establish which is more equal than the other, and from time to time these underground movements break into open warfare.

In these circumstances exchanges of domestic gunfire are by no means rare. An irritable comment by a husband (the "master" of the house?), "I can never find anything when I need it, why can't you keep the place in better order?" will probably elicit the explosion, "This isn't your office, and I'm not your secretary. I've got enough to do without keeping track of your stuff. Why don't you keep it tidy yourself, and then you'd know where to find it?" Or, the other way round, when business is bad a wife may suggest, "You have so much dead wood at the office—why don't you fire some of them?" which will often bring an infuriated retort, "I know how to run my office. You keep out of my business!"

These may seem to be trivial exchanges, but they show that smooth functioning of individual relationships, the bricks and mortar of social order, is difficult when roles are not clearly defined. Most couples, of course, will not express their resentments so rudely, but even if they repress expression of them they will feel them just the same. Pent-up hostility will color their relationship, and may even result in psychological or physical disturbances, or both.

The cultural role of the woman as the *de facto* if not *de jure* head of the household, however, is only one reason for the partial breakdown of hierarchical order in man. Lying beneath the cultural surface is a biological process, the one that has played the most influential part in the gradual emergence of man. It is the slowing down of the rate of development of the human being so that his childhood is the longest and his early helplessness the most complete of any of the mammals.

We have called this process man's infantilization, and we believe it explains many things about ourselves that we think of as being specifically human. Concretely what it accomplishes is the long period of time available for the growth of brain and intelligence, and for the fixing of playful, experimental, and exploratory tendencies. The price we pay is a long period of helplessness during which we are totally dependent upon our mothers, and the subsequent period of lessening helplessness when we are still socially dependent. As a matter of fact in modern societies our long period of biological dependence is further extended by the requirements of an increasing number of years devoted to education so that today, in most Western societies, human mothers have some control over dependent children for a minimum of twenty years, sometimes for as many as almost thirty.

The process of prolonging youthful stages is not confined to man. It is to be seen in other higher primates, most notably in the chimpanzee, which does not reach full growth for some eleven years. However, the young nonhuman primate, although physically and socially immature for long periods, is able to fend for itself after a comparatively short time, while the young human being is not.

What does this role of child raiser mean to the human mother? It means that for about one-third of her life she holds a position of absolute dominance in her relationship with her children, a position of authority that is often continued if her grandchildren are born while she still has dependent younger children in her home. Some husbands both in America and in England show their recognition of this fact by continuing to refer to their wives as "mom," "mum," or "mother" for as long as they live. It is clear that a habit of dominance becomes built in to the human female and sometimes makes it difficult for her to obey the social requirement that she defer to the male.

The mother's domestic dominance has evolutionary as well as social consequences. It has been observed in baboons and in macaques, and most likely is true also of other primates, that maternal dominance is a factor in preventing incest. As Tinbergen has pointed out, "The baby baboon is put in a submissive relationship to its mother when it is weaned. Actually it isn't really the weaning that brings the traumatic break between mother and infant, it's her refusal to let him cling to her back and ride around there. . . . Anyway, when the mother rejects the infant, she puts him in a submissive state, and for the young male that is incompatible with copulation. Therefore, no baboon incest." Thus, by a method almost as automatic as the mechanisms of

flowers that prevent self-pollination, evolutionary ends are served by
the status factor in sexual function.

So strong is the habit of dominance in women that even in Europe
in the Middle Ages, when the ideals of the church equated asceticism
with goodness, and woman was therefore regarded as impure, a few
females broke through the social pattern of male dominance and
emerged as persons of influence, some as leaders. After a long period
of generally brutish social habits following the fall of the Roman
Empire, by about the tenth century most of the ladies of the ruling
knights and kings sat at table with their husbands. By the fourteenth
and fifteenth centuries, as A. Karlen has pointed out, "letters between
husbands and wives showed mutual affection and respect. Literature
and chronicles portrayed women who openly ruled their husbands,
and noble ladies distinguished themselves in Government and the arts
more than any Roman matron." The songs of the troubadours exalted
courtly love. In the *Song of Roland* and in the charming medieval
Aucassin et Nicolette, we have expressions of women as idealized
objects of love, placed on a high pedestal of value. Eleanor of Aqui-
taine brought to England huge territories of France as a dowry and
thereby wielded political influence. Joan of Arc, without any personal
wealth or base of power, was able to raise armies and to lead them in a
political cause.

Other cultures also record individual women who overcame their
generally low status. A short time after the prophet Mohammed
moved from Mecca to Medina, thereby inaugurating the Moslem era,
Ugba ben Nafi, the Arab governor of Tunisia (and founder of the city
of Kairouan in 645 A.D.), made raids over what is now the frontier
between Algeria and Morocco, but as C. Kininmouth has noted, "the
Berbers proved as stubborn an obstacle to Arab expansion as they had
been to Roman. Berber resistance was led by a remarkable woman,
Kahina, the prophetess and queen of the Aures, a camel-herding tribe
from the Sahara." Kahina's fiery leadership balked his raids. Ugba
tried again later by a more southerly route, "but was surprised by
Kahina's men at Biskra where he was killed with most of his force."

Woman's breakthrough into male-oriented social patterns, at first
only a trickle, is today a torrent pouring through the breach in the
dam. So far we have mostly been dealing with social causes leading to
our present situation, but social manifestations rarely appear unless
underlying biological processes promote them.

One of the errors thoughtful persons have made in recent times in their efforts to understand man's behavior is that too much of their research has been in behavioral analogies between man and other primate species. Given the close anatomical relationship between man and other primates, it is natural that this should have been so, but there is a very basic difference between primate species that has been undeservedly overlooked. It is that each species has evolved different social patterns to deal with the central problem in the lives of all: the comparative immaturity of the young at birth and the long period of care they need. Among nonhuman primate species, only the gibbons have evolved family patterns similar to man's, although the little South American titi monkeys also live in monogamous pairs. A form of paternal behavior is, however, displayed among Japanese macaques. When mothers of this species are giving birth to new infants, dominant males will take over the care of certain offspring in their first or second years, caressing, grooming, and protecting them in a kind of adoption, but this is not a family relationship in our sense. The chimpanzee's or the baboon's young, although they do not mature sexually until quite late in their developmental period, are self-reliant earlier than ours, so that they can grow up as part of the social group to which they belong and are not totally dependent on the parent after weaning.

It seems to us that a breeding couple's social arrangements for the care and protection of their immature young are the most central matters in the lives of the adults of any species, and if we are to discover the strengths and weaknesses of the domestic mores of modern man we should seek comparisons with other species that have evolved degrees of male-female bonding approaching ours as a solution to this problem, whether those species are anatomically close to or vastly different from ourselves.

Of course, this is a controversial statement. Yet the point we are making is to a great extent a mechanical one, for where a certain function has to be performed the function itself imposes certain patterns. There are many possible alternative ways for creatures to care for their young, and in the endless variety of nature almost any method one can think of can be found. But one of the ways, and the one that concerns us, is the close bonding of male and female parent that lasts beyond the impregnation of the female and through the birth and care of the young. Where this mechanism has evolved, certain types of behavior are bound to follow, almost regardless of the anatomical structure of the creatures involved.

Let us look at some of the problems the birds must deal with that are similar to our own. Man's central problem is the immature condition in which his young are born, their long period of helplessness, and their even longer periods of dependency and partial dependency. To deal with this problem man's development has been toward close male-female bonding, which allows the burdens of dependence to be shared. This is not to say that other solutions are not possible: the protective pouch of the marsupial is one of them, the production of excessive quantities of young so that some are bound to survive is another, the early development in the young of an ability to feed themselves is a third, group care of the young as epitomized in social insects is a fourth. The birds, in respect to the rearing of their young, have faced problems similar to man's. Their young are born even more immature than his; they are eggs that must be kept at a certain temperature without letup or they will die. After hatching, the nestling is unable to feed itself. It must be fed until its flight feathers develop and it has learned whatever skills it needs to find its own food. In some species this period of a bird's life lasts almost a year, which is a fair proportion of its total life span, although, of course, not nearly so large as man's period of dependency. To meet these problems many birds have evolved family patterns not unlike our own, in which a mated couple stays together and shares the task of raising the young.

If we grant that many species of birds have evolved a way of dealing with their most urgent problem that is not dissimilar to ours, then can we learn anything from their behavior? We believe that some of it, at least, is suggestive.

Influenced by our primate past and by the social conditions that arose in hunting societies, man continued in the male-dominance patterns that had successfully regulated the groups of his simian ancestors. It is quite possible that as early as the time when agriculture-based groups succeeded hunting ones, this pattern became difficult to sustain because the economic role of the female in the agrarian society is less differentiated from the male's. Some erosion of the man's dominant status in such groups may help to explain the extreme subjugation of women in historic times. In ancient Greece, in Rome, in medieval Europe, and in Oriental and Near Eastern countries until our own times, women have been regarded as creatures of a lesser order and treated as chattels. Almost the only understandable explanation for such attitudes is found in the evolutionary development we have referred to: that the lengthening childhood of human beings has made it more difficult for adult males to be confident of their masculinity than for adult females to feel secure in their femininity, and this has led to an overreaction by the male. If we also consider the fact that any creature whose dominant status is challenged will fight tooth and nail to retain it, we may understand the otherwise inexplicable social position of women, upheld by custom and law, in so many societies in the past few thousand years.

Such erosion of the male's dominance as may have begun to take place as agricultural groups became established has certainly continued, and at a far greater rate, in modern cultures. In these, male dominance has ceased to be useful, and it is becoming obsolete.

Let us now come back to the birds. It is true that among their thousands of species many kinds of family patterns and male-female relationships are to be found (as has been the case also of man). There is the pasha relationship of the cockerel to the barnyard hens, the Don Juan relationship of the manakin who is all display and no nest building, and the complete irresponsibility of the cuckoo. But we want to look at those species of birds whose domestic habits have so many similarities to our own that our ordinary terminology makes many references to them. We speak of courting couples as lovebirds, of the newly married as billing and cooing like a pair of turtledoves, of feathering our nests, of our young flying the coop, and so on. In these birds, where male and female mate and then form a domestic unit, dominance is no longer a factor between them. They form a partnership in which duties are shared and status has no place. All dominance impulses are then directed outward in defense of nest or territory, and the couple is a unit. The male dominance urge (and the female, where it exists) has served its purpose once the individual has proved himself superior to other males and therefore entitled to breed. After breeding, much of this type of sexuality is replaced by parental behavior until the young are reared and a new breeding season comes around. In many species the couple survives the rearing of the young and is perpetuated into new breeding periods, sometimes for the lifetime of the birds. In man, of course, since breeding is not confined to seasonal periods, sexual impulses persist alongside the parental ones—a fact which perhaps makes it difficult for humans to be as undeviatingly true to their spouses as are the mated and bonded birds.

We see in our societies today a developing trend toward an equal partnership between men and women in marriage and in social affairs, with competition increasingly relegated to the couple as a unit or to the family as a group vis-à-vis other couples and families. Dominance of the intrasex variety, of course, still holds an important place in our lives, as it does for most higher animals, in the period when we select our mates.

This trend toward male-female equality in human societies is still only a tendency and not an established fact. It has been a long time in preparation, from the days when certain women asserted their equality by force of personality, to the days when the rank and file of women were moved to assert it, as were the suffragettes at the beginning of this century. The resistance, ridicule, and defeat that they often have had to accept seems to be diminishing in our times. Today not a few men agree in principle to the domestic partnership of couples, and even to their equality in the economic field, our equivalent of the shelter-providing and food-seeking role that is also undertaken equally by males and females among many birds.

As we have found, both biological and social factors have contributed to the present state of affairs, and today it may be that we are in a stage of transition between old and new patterns of social order. But whether or not a new order emerges, there is no doubt that now, in our time, we are witnessing a disruption of the old one, and this has led to much discomfort and malfunction in our lives.

It is ironic and sad that it is often just in those couples where each partner has so much to offer, and where their backgrounds and interests have much in common, that a spilling-over of competitiveness between them is likely to occur. The actual unfolding of a domestic scene will put this idea into sharp focus.

Anyone meeting Paul and Sylvia in the course of a social evening would probably think how ideal a couple they seemed. Paul was obviously an intelligent and capable person. He had started out in a comparatively minor position in the legal department of a very prestigious firm, but he was obviously doing well there, and a good career was open to him. Sylvia was also very intelligent, a witty conversationalist and lively personality besides. She held a good editorial position on a large daily newspaper, which added to her self-confidence. But if their party acquaintance could have followed this couple home he would have been astonished by their private life.

Even before they reached home he would have heard Paul accuse

Sylvia of trying to steal the limelight from him, and her casual dismissal of his complaints only served to fan his anger. It became almost routine for him to mock her in a petulant way. He would bat his eyelashes rapidly and imply that she only got attention because she was using feminine wiles and not because she was intelligent. She would call his postparty histrionics childish and ridiculous, and then the fat was really in the fire. By expressing herself in these terms she unwittingly struck his Achilles' heel.

Paul was the youngest of four brothers by quite a large interval and all his life had struggled to be considered their equal and not the baby of the family. Besides this there were many distinguished men in his family—one was a judge, another held high political office, several were wealthy and influential—and his mother always made it plain that her sights were held very high for him. All this had the effect of intensifying natural competitiveness in him, and as a result nothing he did really gratified him. Paul's awareness of his mother's hope that he equal or surpass his family's high achievers made him feel less secure in his own status. He was dissatisfied with his job, although objectively it was a good one and his friends envied him for it.

Sylvia was not really competing with him socially, but she too was naturally a competitive person who had to shine in company. She was the older of two girls. Her father made much of her, she was confident, and she did very well in school, both academically and athletically. She and Paul had met in college, and at that time he felt flattered that she accepted his attentions. He often boasted to his friends about his accomplished girlfriend; not feeling sure of himself, he wore her like a badge of honor. But all this changed shortly after they got married. He became envious of any attention she attracted.

At the beginning of their marriage Paul had enjoyed their sexual relationship, but after a short time he began to feel that the sex act was an obligation that a man had to perform in order not to be the subject of ridicule. While he blamed Sylvia's competitiveness for his lack of ardor, he was really afraid that he might be a failure in this area.

On learning the true state of affairs between this couple, the observer might be inclined to dismiss it as petty bickering between a spoiled young man and a rather overpowering young woman. But the problems of this couple are a microcosm of the dilemma of modern man that is our subject: the subversion of competitiveness between members of the same sex (a useful, indeed essential, mechanism) into competition between members of the opposite sexes, which not only cannot serve any useful purpose, but is destructive of the most basic human relationship.

Some of the difficulties Paul and Sylvia encountered were personal to them and arose out of the conditions of their childhoods already mentioned. Most specialists in human behavior would find these facts sufficient to explain their problems. But, as we can see, there are elements in their case that transcend their individual personalities and are part of the situation confronting modern man, male and female.

Sylvia was a dominant female; her dominance was a part of her attraction to Paul, who, when they met, appeared to be a dominant male. In earlier times, when a woman's life was confined to the domestic sphere, her competitive spirit could only have brought her into conflict with other females. Today domesticity is merely one of woman's sidelines. She participates in other arenas of life and as a result is pitted as an individual, and not as a woman, in a general struggle for status that involves both men and women.

In Paul one can see the modern male's problem of a long childhood of maternal dominance from which he must free himself to become a man. As a consequence he is driven to fight for supremacy over the very person he loves, undermining their relationship. The reason that Paul is resentful of Sylvia's social ability and success, and is envious of it, is that he feels outclassed by her, as though her achievements reduced his status to the second rank. All his competitive drive for status is aroused by this. Sylvia is no longer for him his wife, his love; she is the competitor, the challenger, the one who may put him down, make him feel less. Not being able to win over her, since she is more nimble than he, his only alternative is to attempt to pull her down, to reduce her rank to his, or below his. This struggle affects his intimate life with her in more than one way. He cannot relate to her with tenderness because he is engaged in competition with her. More fundamentally, because of his primate heritage, it is extremely difficult if not impossible for him to perform sexually with a woman to whom he feels subordinate.

Paradoxically, both of them were successful and attractive young people by objective standards. In his later life, Paul's competitive spirit served him well. He was respected professionally and rose to high position. His career successfully followed a basic biological pattern, male-male competition. On the other hand his competitiveness with his wife could not possibly produce any kind of payoff, for what could its outcome possibly be? His subjugation to her, or hers to him? It produced the only thing it possibly could: a bad marriage for two gifted people who appeared to have everything going for them.

The example of Paul and Sylvia shows that the difficulties of a man troubled by feelings of reduced sexuality or impotence do not necessarily originate in his relationship with his wife. Since today, especially in the United States, the "hunter" role is assumed by women as well as by men, the male may find himself in a dominance conflict with another hunter who happens to be female.

It would be bad enough for him if he lost such a conflict with a male counterpart at the office, but to lose in direct competition with a female compounds his confusion and leaves him feeling annihilated. This cannot help but affect his domestic life. Because the social role of the male has been esteemed above that of the female for so long in our racial history, it is doubly humiliating for a man to find himself bested in even competition with a woman.

Gunther was a man who suffered acutely from such a situation. It went so far that he began to show physical symptoms of stress: high blood pressure, attacks of rapid heartbeat, an inclination to drink too much, and an inability to enjoy a normal sex life, although he remained very devoted to his wife.

Gunther was the number two man in a cosmetic manufacturing firm, and he was very happy in that position until his firm brought in a second vice-president equal in rank to himself, who happened to be a woman. He felt, rightly or wrongly, that the president of his company was on closer terms with the new vice-president than the situation called for. "I'm not certain, but I'm almost sure, that they have an affair going," he said. Here again was the recurrent justification: the lack was not in him; the competition was unfair because of her femininity. But as he talked on it became clear that he was afraid she would displace him. He thought that she was bringing more clients to the firm and that the president was beginning to value her more highly than him (diminishing his rank), although he had no objective evidence of this. If his rival had been a man this situation would have been painful enough, but as he came from an extremely male-dominated family the idea of being outranked by a woman was unbearable.

Of course, the man is not the sole sufferer in our era. The woman has her problems too. She educates herself, works, and qualifies as a competent practitioner in a given field. She then often finds that male associates react to her as a female and not as a lawyer, administrator, researcher, or whatever she happens to be. We know of an attractive woman who after her husband's death inherited the ownership and took on the presidency of a freight forwarding concern. Both the firm's vice-presidents thought they could make headway by flirting with her. She was able to retain her rank only because she put their relationship onto a business footing promptly and effectively. Since she was the boss this was comparatively easy for her, but for a female researcher, for example, to explain a useful idea and to have the feeling that her listener is thinking about her figure rather than what she is saying is a very frustrating experience. And what of the feelings of the woman who has worked ably for many years eventually to reach an executive position, and who happens to hear herself being referred to as "that broad," or some equally contemptuous term, by a male subordinate?

In Chapter 6 we referred to the way some animals use their vocabulary of sexual gestures metaphorically, to symbolize nonhostility. Today, what do we find in man? The colloquial verbs that denote sexual activity, which should be the culmination of tender feelings and loving intimacy, are being used to denote contempt and hostility. This use of these verbs has become so general that we hear children uttering them without comprehending their original sexual meaning, only their abusive connotations. It is apparent that a visceral awareness of the disarray of the relationship between the sexes has reached us, before the brains of the scientist and analyst have identified it and interpreted it to us.

We believe that a time must come when it will be possible for the human male to separate his feelings about the masculinity or femininity of his challenger out of his hunting (business) life and confine them to the domestic sphere. Even there, as we have suggested, we believe that an equal partnership between a bonded pair must eventually evolve, leaving social competition where it primarily belongs, in establishing male and female rank for the courting stage and its connected prerogatives. But there is no doubt that in our present world, where rapid transitions are taking place, man must contend with many ambiguities and perplexities.

10

Two Kinds of Love

Human love in all its complexity has its origins in two sources. The first is the parental love we all experience as infants, and the second is sexual drive. In each person these two kinds of love mix in different proportions, resulting in the countless variations on the theme of love that we see in ourselves and in our fellows.

To show the kaleidoscopic nature of the end result—the falling in and out of patterns, the forming of new patterns with the same pieces—this chapter will examine personal stories. In doing so we hope to show how deceptive appearances may be, and how often our conclusions and advice, well intentioned as they may be, are in fact wrong.

When we see people united in a relationship that to us appears totally unsatisfactory, the very fact of their bond may reveal something of the interlocking patterns that overpower the conventional considerations that would judge them unsatisfactory.

Victor

A man we know is successful in his field, esteemed by his clients and colleagues, but frustrated and unfulfilled in his personal relationships. We shall call him Victor.. His problems illustrate vividly how difficult it is to understand any person's behavior without some idea of the biological forces that lie beneath it.

Victor is forty-one and unmarried, although he is always saying how much he would like to settle down and have a family. Some of his happiest days are spent visiting his friends' homes. He enjoys the feeling of being one of a family, and he likes to take their children out for walks or to ball games. Victor is a highly eligible man, well off financially and reasonably good-looking. His friends don't understand why he seems unable to find a wife.

It is only a year since Victor became disenchanted with Audrey, an intimate friend of five years' standing. From the outside it looked as though they had an ideal relationship; his friends assumed that it would end in marriage. He treated her with a great deal of love and respect, and she showed him so much consideration that their friends said she spoiled him. Although she preferred what she called "plain, wholesome food," she soon came to realize that his taste was for the more exotic. So she collected and studied a veritable library of cookbooks, spared no effort in tracking down the special ingredients called for by their recipes, and even took time off from her work to prepare unusual dishes for him and his friends. Once, when they were visiting Audrey's sister's home, her brother-in-law mixed a Bloody Mary for Victor, and she noticed that he added only a dash of Worcestershire sauce to it. Knowing that Victor liked his drink well seasoned, she got up and added more for him. The host laughed and said, "I wish my wife would look after me like that." And then, unlike most golf widows, Audrey never seemed to mind when Victor spent one of his rare free days on the course.

When Victor began to seek the company of other women, his friends were at a loss. One of them asked what went wrong. Victor too seemed perplexed, and appeared to welcome the chance to talk about his problems.

"I'll be damned if I know what I'm doing," he said. "I hate myself for it. I know what I'm doing to Audrey isn't right, but I just don't know what gets into me these days. When I'm with her I get bored. I often fall off to sleep. I can't even blame her. She's always been such a good companion and still is, but I don't seem to be able to work up any interest in what she does or what she says any more. My thoughts wander off. I do my level best—I try to force myself to pay attention to what she is saying, but I can't. I don't seem to be interested sexually either, although there's really nothing I could complain about. She's pretty good, and she tries hard to please me every which way—but I'd just as soon roll over and go to sleep. I tell her I have a lot of business problems, and I'm tired and so on, but I don't really think she believes me, though she's a good sport."

Not long after this conversation he broke off completely with Audrey, and, after a few attempts that led nowhere, he has now become involved with Vicky.

Vicky is as different from Audrey as a human being can be. She is much older than Audrey, she has had a stormy marriage that ended in divorce, and she has two children who are difficult to handle. At times she is winning and full of a sparkling charm that holds men's attention, but at others she is a shrew. She constantly fights with her maids, whom she dismisses in rapid succession, as well as with her children.

Victor's friends are unable to understand his infatuation with her. She is not above using vulgar language, she is not as good-looking as Audrey, and she almost makes it a point to disregard his wishes. In other people's company she often behaves in ways that compel him to make excuses for her later on.

Often, after a few days of relative harmony, she suddenly begins to accuse him of ogling waitresses or chasing other women. At other times she accuses him of being a "closet queen." In these periods she asserts her opinion that no man can be trusted. "You are all bastards," she says to him. She also expresses doubt about his competence in his profession, comparing him to others in the same field she considers way above him. She fights with him. She says she doesn't want to see him any more.

Nevertheless, Victor is completely in the thrall of this woman. When she is not fighting or abusing him he finds her exciting and desirable. He is by no means submissive when she is in an abusive mood; he finds himself using language he is not accustomed to, and this surprises him. He has been even more shocked when once or twice he actually slapped her. But even after such fights, and after her threats to call the police, he still pursues her. She is constantly on his mind, to the point of affecting his efficiency. On several occasions when a break has seemed to be final on her side, he has telephoned her and asked her to marry him.

The conventional psychological explanation for Victor's kind of responses (and there are many others like him) would be to call him a masochist, a person who seeks punishment. But this serves only to provide a label; it doesn't begin to explain the complexity of his behavior. If we now uncover its evolutionary-biological underpinnings, it looks quite different.

Let's take a look at the biological basis of Victor's behavior.

The first bond a human being experiences creates a basis for the ability to have warm and tender feelings. It is, of course, the sensuous bond of mutual feeling, touching, holding, nurture, that is built up between a mother and a child. The infant's first experience of pleasure becomes so deeply embedded (as described in Chapter 3) that it becomes a part of the lifelong response mechanisms that express love.

If some unfortunate circumstance separates an infant from its mother and no loving substitute for her is found, the child grows up unable to express tender feelings, has difficulty relating to other people in friendship, and either cannot rear children of its own or at best can only rear them unsatisfactorily. The now well-known experiments carried out by H. F. and M. K. Harlow confirmed what had been inferred from observation. When a young monkey was reared with an artificial mother made of wire frame constructed to provide the necessary warmth and food, it developed into a withdrawn adult, unable to associate with other monkeys, unable to mate, and spent most of its time crouched in a corner, hugging itself and rocking back and forth. When the conditions were improved, and the artificial mother was padded with cloth so that a young monkey could find some comfort in clinging to it as well as being fed, this young animal when it became adult was capable of associating with others of its kind, although it made a poor parent in its turn. Only when the young monkeys were reared with their natural mothers did they develop normally.

Because humans go through an especially lengthy phase of childhood, mother-child intimacy has even wider ramifications in our species than in any other of the primates, indeed, than in any other species at all. The long helplessness of the human baby has been recognized as the matrix of almost all the thoughts, feelings, and behavior that we think of as specifically human, and experts are increasingly discovering how important are the first three years of a child's life in determining what kind of an adult it will become.

This leads us to the first of the two kinds of love of our chapter title, parental love. What are the biological factors underlying this type of love?

A hormonal output provides a ground from which parental feeling can spring. This is, of course, more marked in the woman, whose hormones in pregnancy, parturition, and lactation have subsidiary effects in creating her inclination to care for the infant. But the man also feels tenderness and concern for the child. It may be said that his feelings are due to cultural influences, because hormonal equivalents have not been detected. But, since parental care-giving is present in not a few other species, it is quite conceivable that more than purely learned behavior underlies it. In them it could be that the temporary cessation of sexual relations enforced by the birth of offspring sets up impulses to give care, but in man such temporary cessations of sexual activity may occur for purely cultural reasons, and so the picture is clouded. Perhaps the sight of the newborn is the trigger to more intensive feelings of wanting to give care, but whatever the promoter of it may be, the feeling is present and manifests itself in many guises. It may have started with an urge to greater food-gathering activity. One has only to observe any male bird with chicks in his nest to see this kind of behavior. Interestingly enough, the original unit of measurement of prolactin was the amount necessary to make an immature male pigeon sit on a nest of eggs. (Prolactin is the hormone that the pituitary gland releases to bring in mother's milk immediately after a baby is born. In pigeons it stimulates milk-secreting glands in the crops of both males and females and promote parental behavior in them. Prolactin is identical in birds and mammals and was first discovered in pigeons.)

Recent research has revealed the extraordinary fact that the brain itself can act like a gland insofar as it has the ability to secrete hormonelike substances. A region at the base of the brain (the hypothalamus) is connected to the pituitary gland by a capillary system through which it releases substances that in turn stimulate (and perhaps also can inhibit) the pituitary in its own hormone production.

The pituitary had been thought of as the master gland, controlling the body's vital functions and setting the stage for the expression of emotions. Now it is learned that this "master" gland in turn is controlled by the glandlike powers of the brain.

In the course of this research the curious fact has emerged that *prolactin is as plentiful in males as it is in females.* To the time of writing the purpose of male prolactin remains a mystery. It is plain that no hormone can be produced by the body without having an effect on some part of the total system, but the effect of male prolactin has not yet been traced. We venture to speculate that when this mystery is solved, prolactin will be shown to play a part in promoting a male's paternal feelings and above all the bonding drive with which these feelings are connected.

As far as the inhibitory factor is concerned, another thought emerges. We know that stress inhibits the growth hormone produced by the pituitary. If male prolactin is the promoter of the bonding drive, and if stress should prove to inhibit its production as well, we should then have a built-in mechanism that could act toward preventing gross overpopulation in man by setting up attitudes of parental indifference. No stretch of imagination would then be required to assume that parental indifference might be preceded by general sexual indifference, a biological ingredient of impotence. Psychologically, stress has been proved to be a factor in impotence. Since stress has been shown to contribute to the regulation of other animal populations, it is possible that it might in certain extremes have a similar role in humans.

Along with the "male" hormone testosterone in women, this evidence of the "female" prolactin in men gives further biological basis to the great overlapping of male and female character traits that tend to militate against the rigid separation of roles in our species.

Whether male birds simply respond to signals by a built-in behavioral mechanism, whether there is a hormone that promotes their responses, whether the ending of the sexual activity of the breeding season is "sublimated" into parental behavior, or whether some combination of these elements is involved is open to question. Equally, whether the human male responds to certain signals, whether a particular hormone promotes his fatherly feelings, whether the damming up of his libido during his wife's confinement or some combination of these factors brings out *his* parental feelings is also open. The fact remains that most men do have protective feelings toward their young and do manifest some degree of paternal behavior.

There is a very ancient custom, found in one or another form almost universally, called *couvade*. This word derives from the French *couver*, meaning "to hatch," and describes practices in which the human male, around the time of the birth of his child, retires to bed, goes through a pantomime of labor, and receives attentions comparable to those given to a woman in childbed.

The practice of couvade was documented in ancient Greece. Strabo reported, "[The women] till the ground, and after parturition, having put their husbands instead of themselves to bed, they wait upon them." Couvade was observed by Marco Polo in Chinese Turkestan, and it has been found in other parts of China as well as in India, Vietnam, Borneo, Thailand, Africa, and the Americas. Among the Mojave Indians, transvestite men traditionally mimicked childbirth and went aside from the camp to be ceremonially delivered of stones. The practice, and the feelings that prompt it, are apparently deep-rooted, for it appears in Greek mythology in the legend of the birth of Athena from Zeus's head, and in the tale of Zeus sewing the fetus of Dionysus into his own loins, carrying it to term, and giving birth to the young god. The twelfth-century French romance, *Aucassin et Nicolette,* tells how the hero found himself in Carthage, where he asked for the king. He was told that the king lay in childbed. When he then asked about the king's wife, "they told him that she was with the army [where she was leading] all the folks of the land."

Several interpretations have been offered for this widely dispersed custom and for the essentially parallel rites that are obligatory for the father at the time of birth in tribal societies. Some see in them a ceremonial means for the father to identify himself with the child. Others see it more as a desire to savor all the possibilities of life. Yet others suggest that men thus express elements of unconscious guilt, hostility, and the desire to atone for those feelings. Several psychologists have suggested that men envy the woman's ability to bear a child. Bruno Bettelheim thought the man tries to detract from the woman's importance, and Gregory Zilborg spoke of his need to subjugate her. Margaret Mead has called attention to the "rebirth" aspect of the boys' initiation rites in New Guinea,

> where the men build great men's houses which they call wombs; they go through elaborate ceremonies of giving birth to the initiate so that when the boys are a certain age they will be taken over by the men and fed on the men's blood, which makes them children of the men. . . . In a large number of these ceremonies the entire ritual is a way of asserting that men are really the creators of children; that they, not the women, are the makers of men.

The modern vogue for the father to be present and sometimes assist during the birth of his child has also been considered an expression of this need. However, if we look again at a father bird taking his turn incubating his eggs, behavior that surely has a hormonal base, we may wonder whether the human father's apparent need to express his identification with his infant and his part in its production does not also have a biological underpinning.

The sight of new fathers gazing with pride at their new offspring from behind the aseptic glass panel of a modern hospital is a familiar one, and it suggests that perhaps it is the actual sight of the squirming newborn that acts as a "releaser" to paternal feelings, much as the "begging" or "soliciting" behavior of nestlings releases parental behavior in several species of birds. It may even be that paternal feelings are "released" still earlier in the cycle by some means not yet considered. The fact that a sizable proportion of prospective fathers experience pregnancy symptoms (including nausea, vomiting, fainting, leg cramps, back pains) would suggest that the sight of their pregnant wife is a possible "releaser."

Whatever the means by which human maternal and paternal behavior is triggered, it plays such a fundamental and pervasive role in a child's development that it becomes an integral part of its personality as it develops and becomes an adult. Let us take a closer look at mothering and fathering so that we can see what they consist of, what they cause directly, and what are their wider ramifications.

In mammals and birds, we see a relationship between two creatures, one mature and strong, the other immature and weak, in which the strong creature takes no advantage of its superior strength but on the contrary sustains and protects the weak one. This may look like a very obvious observation, and so it is where parents and their young are concerned. It becomes remarkable in man only when, as we shall see, this kind of behavior becomes transferred to other adults.

Not only does the strong animal feed and care for the weak one, but all the hostile impulses that adults of the same species normally display when one approaches too closely to another or when competition of any kind is involved are suspended, but only for the weak creature. Further, the strong animal will even suspend its deepest instinct for self-preservation and risk its own life in defense of the weak one. These dramatic inhibitions of the self-protective drives are made possible by hormones. This is completely clear and demonstrable in the female, and we have to assume that there is a hormonal basis for the male's behavior since we know that "mood" is established by hormonal production.

In man, mothering and fathering have to go on for so long that they become an integral part of our behavior patterns as adults. Slowly, evolutionary processes have selected those who show the greatest propensity for giving selfless care to the long-defenseless young. So deep a part of our nature has this become that even when the mating drive, with its totally different responses, emerges during adolescence, it only displaces the parentalistic tendency for a limited time and to varying degrees (as we shall come to immediately). This makes for the enormous complexity of human love.

We cannot leave the subject of parental (tender) love without mentioning some of its profound extensions. The ideas that inspire what we consider to be the highest levels of human action stem from this ability for the prolonged care of the defenseless child. We feel that it is right and necessary to care for all weak creatures, for the poor, the sick, and, recently, for minorities, and for all those suffering from any kind of disadvantage. These extensions of parental love are perhaps fairly obvious. But it goes further. It forms the basis for the ability to experience tender feelings altogether, and so it underlies romantic love, some kinds of friendship, and many forms of self-sacrifice.

The second kind of love of our chapter title is the one that springs from sexual drive. Everybody knows the difference between a man and a woman being "in love" and the love one feels for parents, friends, and children. The feelings are different, the behavior that accompanies the feelings is different, and the feelings arise from different sources. We need different words to describe the two separate sensations, but we usually modify the big umbrella word, *love,* with an adjective to indicate what we mean.

But words are expressions of human thoughts and feelings. They do not arise in our language unless there is a reason for them, and indeed there is an overlapping between tender love and passionate love. We turn our attention now to the biological forces that give rise to sexual love.

As young bodies mature in preparation for breeding, a whole symphony of biological forces comes into play. As the young male develops, the aggressiveness that is part of his sexuality becomes the predominant theme. This aggressiveness serves many vital purposes: it ensures that breeding is performed by the "fit," it prepares the new generation to take over from the preceding one, and it supports the activity necessary to sustain the young that are about to be created. The young female's body undergoes profound changes that prepare her for mating and for reproduction, and these changes are all part of the broader aspects of her sexuality. This is the phase when the "male" sex hormones produced by both male and female take over the symphony, incorporating the earlier themes. In the well-balanced human being all the motifs—aggression, tenderness, sexuality, love, and competitiveness—intermingle, counterpointing the dominant theme of sexual love. There is sufficient latitude in the mingling of all the components to allow for many variations in normal human sexuality, but if an undue stress on any one element occurs it strikes us as a dissonance and, if it is very extreme, as a cacophony.

Underlying this complexity is an urgent **drive** toward the simple goal of uniting two bodies. The vascular congestion of the genital organs makes imperative demands. Aggression plays a significant role, although in our culture it is only in unusual circumstances that it finds its original outlets. Usually it becomes incorporated into socially acceptable forms no longer recognizable as expressions of an aggressive drive. It may be competition for better jobs, or studying for better grades, so that young males may qualify themselves to gain wives and eventually raise families, or so that young females may attract mates, be better-qualified wives and mothers, and sometimes help support their families.

This is our equivalent of the intrasex competition of other species. What we see as the innocuous and laudable endeavor of the student to excel is nothing more or less than a cultural continuation of the physical battle for dominance. We take these activities for granted and usually do not realize that they require a great deal of energy, which is supported by hormonally conditioned aggressiveness. We have only to put ourselves into the shoes of a depressed or withdrawn person (who is deficient in this drive) to discover how much of an effort it is to perform even the simplest social obligations. All the activities we think of as preparation for adult life serve to fit the young person for the essential business of maturity, which is procreation.

Although we are describing these two kinds of love separately, many of the characteristics that should distinguish one from the other overlap. When we speak of a drive for the union of two bodies we may be describing the sexual act or the clinging of the infant to its mother. In a way there is also an interpenetration between a suckling baby and its nursing mother, insofar as an organ of one is taken into an organ of the other and liquids are exchanged. When we think of desire for closeness between a man and a woman, who can deny that the child has a desire for closeness with its mother? The tender love a parent feels for a child is also a part of the love relationship between man and woman. Even aggression is a part of parental love as well as of sexuality. Parents will fight to protect their young; lovers of either sex ward off competition. It is only when one element of love predominates unduly that a disturbed relationship results. And this brings us back to Victor and the reason his predicament is so illuminating.

For reasons that arose out of disruptions in his early rearing, and that would be beyond the scope of our theme to detail here, the elements of mature love did not coalesce in Victor as he became adult. The same factors caused him to be a lonely and shy adolescent. It was only when he began to make headway in his profession that he found women were attracted to him, and he became emboldened to seek them out. After a number of short-lived affairs he settled down with Audrey. At that time she fulfilled a deep longing in him that must have been frustrated since his earliest youth. She was warm and protective and tender, and he responded to her in about the same way as a child would to its mother.

Of course, he was oblivious to the nature of the relationship. He found comfort in her physical closeness, in the care she took of him, and in the attention she gave him. So far as he was concerned it seemed to be a normal relationship between a man and a woman with love on both sides.

Initially his feeling of well-being with Audrey aroused him sexually, but as time went on his biological response mechanisms approximated more and more those of an infant to a mother and less and less those of a man to a mate. After being fed and tended by its mother, an infant falls into a blissful sleep. In the early days of his relationship with Audrey when Victor fell asleep in her arms he was very grateful, for he felt she gave him a release from the pressures of his daily work. It was only later that he became aware that there was something amiss in falling asleep in the arms of a pretty woman without any sexual arousal. There was no excitement in their relationship; as he put it, there was no "zing." Not surprisingly, his feeling of boredom increased as he became more successful professionally. To us, it is now apparent that the competitiveness and aggression aroused by his professional challenges set into motion hormonal responses that activated sexuality. That is to say, his love needs became weighted less toward tender expression and more toward the type of sexuality associated with the drive to breed.

After the arousal of aggressiveness in his professional activities, his chance meeting with Vicky opened the door for this drive to enter into his sex life. His intellect told him that Vicky did not offer a good relationship, but he found that fighting with her stimulated him sexually, and this perplexed and distressed him. He couldn't help thinking how much better he had had life with Audrey. And yet he was bored with her.

Victor's experience is far from unique. Very often men who started in business in a small way but then rose rapidly gradually find their wives less interesting and less sexually stimulating. In their earlier years together they were happy. The companionship, warmth, and tender love were exactly what they needed at the time when their economic positions were low. But once a stronger competitive drive was aroused and, feeding on itself, led to greater successes, their responses shifted away from the noncompetitive warm relationship. As the need to fight, to win, to conquer took over and was accompanied by an increased production of sex hormones, their sexuality moved to the other end of the spectrum. Now, to keep it sparked, it needed an element of aggression. They are then driven to seek struggle. The love that stems from the early nursing period no longer gratifies them. They seek the kind of sexual challenge that goes with their aroused combativeness and feel stimulated by women who present them with this challenge.

This urge, when it is experienced, is very compelling. Everything else is flat in comparison. Men, and women too for that matter, abandon secure positions in their communities, family relationships, and may go so far as even to abandon their children; they are driven by everything in them to satisfy this new need. This might be called the "hormonal reason" that explains what is almost a cliché of our culture: the successful man indulging in what is usually thought of as a "last fling."

As he does so he can hear a chorus buzzing in his ears: "Whatever got into him?" "Is he crazy?" "What does he expect to get from a girl like that? She's nothing but a gold digger, she'll give him a hell of a time. . . ." But, as often as not, it is not the desire to hold on to youth that precipitates his "madness," but the hormonal concomitant of his personal success.

The usual assumption that the new woman has enticed the man by superior sexual prowess is not borne out objectively. The challenge of the new experience provides an intensity to the man's sexual arousal, and the difference is in *his* sexual performance, rather than in any difference between the two women.

Victor's attraction to Vicky now becomes more understandable. He met her at a time when his professional life was reaching a peak (his status increasing by many rungs), and he found a need for his personal life to keep pace with the excitement of his daily occupations. The blandness of his social life with Audrey was no longer a welcome respite, but an unappreciated tedium. The submissive role he had played in earlier days had changed into a dominant one, as was reflected in his hormone production and in his behavior—that is to say, in his entire set of neurophysiological responses. Although his mind tells him that the constant battling with Vicky is undesirable by his own social standards, his body, primed for aggressive competition, just charges in and enjoys the struggle.

An important element in the elation Victor feels in his relationship with Vicky is below the surface, unspoken, and probably unrealized. It is the constant struggle between them as to which will "master" the other—that is, dominate or control their life together. When Vicky "puts him down" by casting aspersions on his professional ability ("You were just lucky to get where you are") and on his masculinity ("What's so attractive about those boys?"), she is attacking him in the areas that determine status. Instinctually she aims at the vital spots and thereby asserts her own superior rank. When Victor interferes in her domestic arrangements, speaks up for her children, or tries to smooth out her quarrels with her maids, she senses that he is trying to take over *her* authority and dominate her life. At the heart of their relationship is a battle for dominance, and although at times it seems almost more than either of them can bear, it stimulates them and gives them a feeling of being excitingly alive—a feeling that forges the bond between them.

To outsiders it is mystifying how such a relationship can continue. But an outsider is not aware of the underlying forces that bind these people together. Important to their satisfaction is the fact that they are evenly matched. If she were weaker he would crush her—and lose his opponent. If she were able to dominate him, she would have the field to herself, and no battle. The winner would become bored and the loser depressed. Strangely enough, the view of the outsider notwithstanding, an evenly matched sparring couple like Victor and Vicky has a better chance of remaining together than many a more peaceful one.

It should not be thought that we are recommending this kind of relationship. We are describing it because it offers such a good illustration of the biological forces we have been writing about. While it is not a very common basis for a successful marriage (because people rarely show a single drive so clearly; more often many drives intermingle), it is also not an extremely uncommon one.

It would appear that a need for dominance would be more important to the man, in his role as breadwinner and supporter of the family, than for the woman. But this is not at all the case. Very often, even in cultures where it is the norm for the man to be considered to "head" the family, the realities of individual family lives are the other way around. Strong matriarchal influence is accepted among many groups, but it often exists even where it is not. We then find groups of "dominated" men escaping their homes and assembling in local cafes, bars, clubs, or at stag parties, and bolstering each other's egos with fantasied heroics. The subjects of their boasting are revealing, for they most often talk about their successes with women, their experiences in war or fights, or tell off-color jokes that "put down" women.

Throughout nature there are many species besides our own in which hierarchies of rank are as marked among the females as among the males. Therefore it is not surprising that competitiveness should be as apparent in the female of our own species as in the male, especially since relatively late in primate evolution females have developed a biological factor capable of triggering competitiveness along with sexuality in the same way as in males. That is the influence of the male hormone she produces, a strong factor in her sexual receptiveness.

Of course, the competitiveness triggered by the "male" hormone in women may be greatly modified by the hormones promoting maternal responses. Thus there is a potential for either, or both, types of behavior in women, and for an infinite number of gradations between them. Perhaps because the emergence of the male component as a factor in femininity is a relatively late evolutionary development, this element is still in a transitional stage, and there may be some seesawing between the maternal and the aggressive components of femininity in our species.

Many women are wholly maternal in their feelings, not only toward their children, but also toward their husbands. They express their love by caring for their husbands' bodily needs, feeding them, tending them, supporting their aspirations, offering advice and guidance when necessary, making their surroundings pleasant, and always being available for comfort or solace. They are the women who say to each other, "All men are big children," and that is indeed the true basis of their feelings for them. In Victor's life such women were epitomized by Audrey.

But there are other women who find great stimulation in the company of men, and this stimulation has nothing of a maternal quality. We are not here speaking only of the women who openly compete with men in business and professional fields, but of those who enjoy a good conversation; whose whole manner becomes animated, whose interest is aroused, who are vivacious and seem to become a little more alive when they become involved in an intellectual discussion, or even in social banter. Unlike Vicky, these women do not need to fight to obtain satisfaction for their "aggressive-competitive" status drives. In them the contest is masked in conventional forms, but its biological basis is the same. Such women do not "mother" their husbands. They think of them as companions; they enjoy taking part in the same activities and take pleasure in pulling equal weight whatever the mutual endeavor. They feel alive when they are participating in exchanges of ideas or sharing work, and they feel dull or bored when they are without this stimulus. Although we do not yet have any concrete evidence to prove it, it seems likely that this type of female behavior also is mediated by the male component of their sexuality.

In all likelihood this "new" male factor is not as firmly embedded in women as the evolutionarily older maternal one. It is a matter for speculation as to why this development should have occurred in primates, what selective advantages it afforded, and to what end it is leading our species. Will it eventually tend to eliminate or blur sexual dimorphism? Is our current trend toward the erosion of differences in social sex roles based on this biological fact, and does it indicate the direction in which we are headed? All we actually see at the moment is a potential in all primates that appears to be becoming an actuality only in man.

Carla

The kind of transformation that occurred in Victor's life may also happen in the life of a woman, although we discern it less clearly in women because of cultural prejudices. A person we shall call Carla reflects a mirror image of Victor, modified only by the difference in stakes that on the whole seem more appropriate to a woman in our culture.

Carla had the kind of mind that avidly absorbed any subject that came her way, and she pursued a wide variety of interests. In school she had excelled without effort. However, the social pressures of her time and place were so great that when she was twenty-one she made a conventional marriage to a banker considerably older than she.

At first she threw herself wholeheartedly into what she considered to be the duties of her marriage. She established a beautiful home and devoted a lot of attention to making sure that at any time of day or night an unexpected visitor would find ready hospitality in well-organized and esthetically pleasing surroundings. She spent a great deal of time entertaining her husband's business associates. Her own interests and intellectual curiosity were relegated to her private time. She satisfied them as well as she could with extensive reading and, sometimes, with independent travel.

Nevertheless, after a few years of this life she became aware of a growing sense of restlessness and discontent, which she managed to conceal. She realized that everyone who knew her thought she led an ideal existence: a beautiful home, no financial worries, and a devoted husband in a prestige profession. "What more do you want?" her friends would have said if she had revealed her state of mind. Indeed, she asked herself the same question.

When her children were born after some years, they became a focus for her interest, and all her energies were diverted to them, but still she was acutely aware that her great need for intellectual stimulation remained unsatisfied. As her children grew older and needed her less she found herself withdrawing more and more from her husband on every level. She ran their home, but more perfunctorily. Whenever her children needed her she gave them the best of her knowledge, experience, and feelings. But she began to live a private life. She made friends of her own; started to attend courses to bring herself up-to-date in the subjects she had studied in her youth; attended art classes to find an outlet for her creativeness; and traveled alone or with a woman friend more frequently.

This went on for about ten years. Carla resigned herself to her life and made up her mind to make the best of it. But nevertheless from time to time she was overcome with feelings of despair, that her life had been a terrible waste, but without really knowing where she had taken a wrong turn nor what she could do. Day-to-day conversations with her husband became so tedious to her that the only way she could sustain them, or for that matter her entire relationship with him, was by closing her feelings off and separating her inner world from the world of her daily existence.

It was at this stage that Carla called on a family friend whose husband was a professor of sociology. Her own husband found his conversation too pedantic and after the first time did not accompany her, but she enjoyed it and repeated the visit occasionally in the evenings. She found the discussions interesting and discovered a sense of coming back to life in the debates that arose out of them. This professor, outside his academic duties, was engaged in a project with a highly successful professional man who also had a wide range of interest and knowledge, and whom we shall call Mark. It occurred to the professor that Carla might enjoy participating in some of their discussions, and so one evening Carla met Mark.

The effect was electric. Unlike the professor, who had carried on very gentlemanly debates with her, Mark was an intellectual "slugger." He took strong stands on controversial issues and had no inhibitions about ramming home his points. Carla joined the fray and found herself participating with a degree of excitement that she had not felt since the years before her marriage.

When she went home her mind was full of this man. On one hand she felt him to be overbearing and a trifle too imbued with his own convictions, but on the other she felt such a sense of elation that she could hardly sleep. All night she went over in her mind the points that had come up during the discussion, thinking of new ones she could have made. When Mark telephoned her a few days later she was eager to continue the verbal battle.

They met, took a stroll in a nearby botanical garden. In their conversation she reverted to a particular point he had made on the evening they had first met and on which she emphatically disagreed with him. He took up the argument, and then they both vigorously supported their own views. Suddenly, as if from nowhere, she experienced an overwhelming physical attraction to this man, whom she hardly knew.

It was at their next meeting, to which she went with a distinct sense of foreboding, that it happened: unthinkingly, at the age of about fifty, Carla plunged into an affair. All thoughts of consequences, of the beliefs and values she had upheld for a lifetime, were swept away. The sexual excitement she experienced matched the pitch of the intellectual excitement.

The transformation in Carla escaped no one, except perhaps her husband. She became more vivacious. Her friends commented that she looked years younger. She began to undertake enterprises that she had resigned herself to putting out of her life when she married and, at that late stage, began the professional career she had contemplated as a young person but never entered. Her own new-found drive obtained an added impetus from her pleasure in involving herself in Mark's interests and activities and no slight fillip from the sense of competitiveness he aroused in her. In a surprisingly short time she began to receive professional recognition, which she found very gratifying.

It wouldn't be too difficult to find a conventional psychological explanation for Carla's character makeup. Having been forced by a tradition-minded, rather stern and distant father to abandon thoughts of a career in favor of early marriage, she had eschewed independent adult fulfillment and found a man considerably her senior who offered the kind of warmth that her father had not shown her. This would explain the gradual diminution of sexual interest in her marriage, because the incestuous overtones of the relationship were very close to the surface.

As in the case of Victor, this conventional explanation, valid as it is in its own terms, doesn't begin to reveal the chain of deep-seated biological responses that were involved in Carla's transformation.

If unchecked, Carla's personality would have impelled her aggressive spirit and sexuality into a career and a passionate love. Parental authority and social pressure effectively balked this tendency and redirected her toward a marriage in which her sexuality and competitiveness were blunted. Like Victor with Audrey, the love she found was of the type that derives from parental protection. Like Victor, she soon found it dulling all her responses. And like Victor her aggressive spirit was driven underground, only occasionally surfacing in the diversions she engineered for herself and only fully emerging under the impact of her meeting with Mark.

This meeting struck a spark that set in motion a whole series of hormonal responses. Competitiveness, sexuality, aggressiveness, all were awakened, acted upon each other, and ultimately effected a total change in her life. One can see in this a duplication of the changes that take place in nature at the time of the mating season. In Carla the sequence of hormonal preparations for mating were aroused belatedly at the age of fifty. What she had experienced before, including her sexuality, was a persistence of (or a reversal to) an infant's response to love. In retrospect it seems rather obvious that once this process was aroused everything in her life fell into place. Under the constant stimulation of the new relationship she not only took on a professional life, but also takes great pleasure in joining Mark in strenuous sports activities. She rises at what previously would have been unheard of hours so as to be able to accomplish everything she sets herself to do. She remains a living example of the close connection between energy and adult sexual love.

This theme has many variations. The personal stories recounted in this chapter represent the extreme corners of the possible configurations. In the next example a reverse process took place, and it shows how the transformation of adult sexual love into more parental tender love can sometimes have a devastating effect upon the recipient, who is forced into a childlike, or even an infantile response.

Allen

Just as the "male" quality of aggression is a part of female sexuality, so is the "female" quality of tenderness a part of masculinity. Every human male has some degree of tender love mixed with his aggressive love, else it would not be possible for him to give care as a parent, but in some men this feeling dominates so as to render them almost maternal in the type of love they give. There are very few of us who do not know at least one man whose joy is to do everything for his wife: to provide for her, to pet and spoil her, to think for her, and to try to relieve her of every burden. Among the several we know is a man called Allen.

Allen, a college professor, taught political science. He was married, and his wife was a successful lawyer who had expanded her practice throughout the years of their marriage. They had met as students, when each had a great respect for the other's abilities. So far as his wife was concerned their marriage was perfectly satisfactory and provided an ideal background for her professional life. For Allen, though, there were often nagging thoughts that his salary didn't begin to compare with hers, and he felt uncomfortable when she provided the lion's share of any larger expenses. About midway in his career Allen decided to transfer to government service, hoping to be able to use it as a steppingstone to an eventual lucrative position as a consultant in private industry.

But Allen was basically a gentle person. He had neither the inclination nor the skill in using his elbows to get ahead in the strongly competitive hierarchies of the academic and governmental worlds. He achieved a good upper-middle rank and then seemed to be stuck there, without much hope of reaching the top.

In the long run he became rather discouraged about his career, and his generalized feeling of dissatisfaction began to show in his life. Earlier he had enjoyed brisk walks in all weather and an occasional game of tennis, but now he lost his zest for exercise and preferred to retreat to his library in his spare time. He became aware of a cooling in his feelings for his wife and his lack of any real desire for intimacy with her.

This rather low frame of mind was his mood when Aimee was hired as a secretary in his department four years ago. Aimee had grown up in California. As a girl she had been lovely and dreamed of becoming a film star. She had managed to become part of a circle that existed on the fringes of the film industry, but she had never made it into the enchanted world and had settled for a job as a secretary in a director's office. Later she married, but her unrealistic fantasies of glory undermined the marriage. It crumbled after a few years, leaving her with two children, very little money (her ex-husband disappeared and made no provision for her), and a host of other problems: men, debts, the education of her children, and her own dreams.

Although she was in her forties by the time she crossed Allen's path, her early beauty was still apparent. He found her attractive, even glamorous, and when he saw her in the cafeteria at lunchtime he got into the habit of inviting her to join him. On these occasions she began to confide in him, to tell him of her problems. Pretty soon he slid into helping her out of her tangled affairs.

For whatever he did for her she showered him with thanks that to an outsider must have seemed almost effusive, but Allen felt a glow kindled by her appreciation and her expressed admiration. She was not above using abysmal clichés and baby talk on the order of "What would poor little me do without you?" or to announcing in loud tones to all and sundry (but in his presence), "Allen is the most brilliant man in the whole service."

Far from being embarrassed by these accolades, Allen soaked them up. They were balm to his wounded spirit. Here was a man who had been a brilliant student, had had high hopes for an impressive career, but who had found himself thwarted, unable to make the grade, outperformed by his wife. Aimee's almost slavish admiration, inappropriate as it may have been, brought back to him a sense of being alive. Her childishly seductive wiles met an instant response in him. He thought her beautiful, intelligent. He was sexually aroused by her and by now has left his wife and moved into Aimee's apartment and life, as he believed, permanently.

But what has happened to Aimee in these last three years that they have been living together?

The first change took place when she asked to be transferred to another department. She suggested, and he agreed, that it would be better for her to work somewhere else, since knowledge of their relationship might cause unnecessary problems in their department. She was transferred, but after a short while she declared she did not like the people in the new office and she was going to look for a job in a business organization. The first step (giving up her government job) was taken, but the second (finding another) never materialized. She made the rounds of employment agencies, got work for which she was unsuited, either was dismissed within a few days or left of her own accord. She took on temporary, even daily and hourly work, and found this too great a strain. Now she stays around the house more and more, saying that she finds the pilgrimages to the agencies and interviews depressing and tiring.

Her health has begun to deteriorate. At first she suffered repeated colds and minor infections, but these have now given way to more serious disorders for which doctors can find no physical basis. She has had dizzy spells. Her legs buckle. At times her gait is so wobbly that she appears to be tipsy although she is not. She complains she has no appetite and, in his presence at least, eats so little that he has taken to feeding her morsels from his own plate. Nevertheless she has gained weight and her stomach is often distended. She has frequently fallen in the street. Although no bones have been broken she has been badly bruised and has remained in bed, or at home, for months on end.

Allen has lost most of his friends because of the inanities of Aimee's conversation and her insistence on making herself the center of attention. But his devotion to her remains unabated. He hurries home from work to cook for her, he does the shopping for her on the way, he washes up and tidies for her, and he telephones her every couple of hours during his working day to make sure that she is all right. It seems strange that all this has not affected his feeling for her. His sense of her absolute dependence on him seems to have intensified the pleasure he derives from their intimacies, which have proceeded undiminished in spite of her many infirmities. To their few remaining friends, indeed, she talks about this quite unblushingly, almost with the same lack of concern with which a four-year-old discusses his bodily functions.

Although this seems to be an extreme example, it is but one of numerous similar couples we have encountered. One man, married to a very petite and frail woman, literally picks her up and carries her in his arms to protect her from the effort of walking. In another couple, where the woman has neurotic fears, her husband caters to her every whim uncomplainingly; it is his duty. In a third the wife is crippled with arthritis, yet her husband's love for her seems to be intensified by the obligation he feels to take care of her. In a fourth the wife is an actress whose career never reached the heights she had hoped for and has now petered out entirely, while her husband, an actor, goes from strength to strength. She has been so deeply hurt by her failure that all his protective instincts have been aroused, and his efforts to shield her from her own emotional pain go beyond any usual response—with the result that the wife is being reduced to a state of dependency almost as extreme as Aimee's and against which she is now ineffectively rebelling. A fifth husband is so occupied with attempting to relieve every member of his family of every small burden (he even goes so far as to spare his wife the dilemma of selecting a menu for the evening meal) that we refer to him privately as the clucking mother hen.

And that, in essence, is at the heart of this kind of behavior. The men concerned have a very high proportion of parental feeling in their love. They feel fulfilled when their wives and families are dependent on them. This gives them a sense of their importance, a feeling of status, and in these circumstances they are "turned on" sexually. When, on the other hand, they happen to marry women who do not need their support, who are capable of independent spirit and able to be equal partners and companions, such men have an inner sense of not being needed. Their glands react to this with responses suitable to lowered status, so that they feel constant mild depression and their sexuality diminishes, like that of a nondominant herd animal relegated to the fringes of its group.

In some instances such relationships work out very well for all concerned, but more often they produce disastrous consequences for the adult recipient of the care-giving type of love. Aimee shows a classical response to it. Inherently she had many immature emotional responses, but she *had* been able to cope with life fairly adequately until she met Allen. She had managed to support herself and her two children and had even helped one of them through college. But with Allen on the scene the necessity for her to cope with her problems was removed. Step by step she has relinquished all responsibility, first for her own support, then for adult duties, and now finally for her own health and well-being. In this last stage her responses are rather complex. On the one hand she wishes to be in fact the helpless child that inside she feels herself to be, but on the other she knows that other people will not accept that kind of behavior from a woman of her age. Her body has found a way to express her feelings about herself. Her giddiness, frequent falling, and wobbly knees reflect the unsure gait of a toddler; her poor appetite gives reason to be fed and coaxed; and her reversion to baby talk tells its own story. It would seem difficult to place adult sexuality within the context of such a childlike reaction, but, to her, sexual relations are on a par with other body functions; and then, there is a brand of sexuality that occurs in the course of every child's normal development. (In this connection it is of interest that ovaries reach their full adult size, although not their mature function, by the time a girl is five.) Aimee satisfied Allen's emotional needs with her dependence, and, as a child finds ways to please its mother so as to be sure of her attention, so she sensed her sexual function as a way to bind him still closer to her. Within the space of about two years this self-supporting and perfectly healthy if emotionally immature woman became physically and socially helpless, and she remains so to this day.

In Allen we have a particularly good example of what can happen to a person who is married to one who is either overly domineering or who is more successful. His feeling of his standing as a man was diminished by his wife's superior accomplishment. His sense of lowered status then probably had the effect of reducing his adrenalin production, since his observable behavior showed a reduction in the drive associated with sexuality and therefore a proportional increase in his need to express love by giving tender care. This effect operates in women as well as in men, although in our cultural climate we notice it more readily in males, since we expect more aggressive behavior from them. We find it less remarkable when a woman shows a reduction in drive. Nevertheless, among our own acquaintances is a woman whose own drive raised her from an impoverished background to a high social position as the wife of a very successful and ambitious doctor who was temperamentally extremely domineering. Under the impact of this marriage her sense of status as a woman has diminished to a point where she has become a childlike creature, kittenish in her behavior, and totally dependent on her husband's direction for every detail of her life. As a result she suffers from recurring depressions which she is unable to understand, since she has achieved everything she strove for.

When we say a reduction in adrenalin production in response to loss of status is responsible for the changes that have taken place in these people, we should mention that the differences in hormonal output are probably minute, perhaps not even measurable by the comparatively crude means that are available to us. Multiplying the difficulties of any measuring attempt would be the constant fluctuations of hormonal rates in response to environmental circumstances; and what would be relevant here would be only a median base rate. All the same, we may fairly assume such changes on the basis of the behavior we can observe in the individuals concerned.

This brings us to another point. None of the people mentioned above can be said to have been made "unhappy" by the changes that have taken place in their lives. The individuals' hormonal responses have actually transformed them into the new people they now are, and they cannot act or feel differently from the way they do. Only if the circumstances of their lives should afford them an opportunity to regain a feeling of status (for instance, by close association with others weaker than themselves) would it be possible for their original drive and independence to be restored.

What, then, constitutes a basis for an harmonious male-female relationship? We are forced to the conclusion that this is not determinable from the outside. Victor's relationship with Vicky, and Allen's with Aimee, look disastrous to any outsider; yet each fulfills the innermost needs of the people concerned. Not one of them would voluntarily give up his or her relationship even if it were pointed out how great the price each is paying to sustain it. The cementing force acts on a lock and key principle. The personality of each fits so precisely into the needs of the other that together each couple forms a binding unity capable of withstanding almost any disruptive force from the outside. Of these there are plenty. Well-meaning friends and relatives have not minced words in pointing out the penalties involved in each relationship. Allen's health is suffering from the strain of maintaining his professional obligations while remaining at Aimee's beck and call. His financial reserves are depleted by her mounting medical bills, her need for domestic assistance, and her relinquished earning power. His social life, which meant a lot to him, is grinding to a halt as one after another of his friends decides he can no longer stand an evening with Aimee. Allen is aware of these things but cannot bring himself to give her up. Aimee herself has been told that her health would improve if she would get back to work, do more for herself, and give Allen more time to pursue his career, but she does not believe it. She thinks she could not survive if he left her alone only for a few days. All Victor's friends have told him he "must be crazy" to tie himself to such a shrewish woman as Vicky when Audrey is so delightful, would make him such a wonderful wife, and is still available. He agrees, yet nothing can tear him from Vicky. Carla too, who had a very orderly existence, a smoothly running household, and the kind of life that her friends considered normal, was warned not to sacrifice all this for the sake of a passing impetuosity. In her case the change has worked out well, and her new marriage has been productive and satisfying since neither personality saps the other, but she did not know this in advance and took the plunge anyway.

Plainly, outsiders who criticize these relationships have an ideal in their minds. Perhaps the ideal derives from childhood stories that end with the words "and they lived happily ever after" or from the even earlier feelings of peace of the suckling infant. But we discover that life does not always reflect our ideals. We find bonds between those whose sexual and status needs tie them together in apparent disharmony as indissoluble as between those who are bound by tenderness and live in harmony. As William Blake wrote, "Man was made for joy and woe." We see that the achievement of status and vigorous sex may sometimes bring in its train a kind of life that many of us would not envy, and yet we cannot say: the price is too high. We cannot even say whether it is desirable or not desirable, good or bad. All we can say is that this is how life is. We may or may not desire it; we may or may not approve of it; all we can do is observe it and, if we will, understand it.

The evidence is compelling that two fundamentally different kinds of love govern human adult sexuality. The first is the love that gives concern, care, tenderness, and has its source in the maternal protection we all experience as infants. The second has its source in the sexual drive of the mating urge.

Neither of these two kinds of love is an exclusively male nor an exclusively female attribute. Both males and females normally possess elements of each kind blended in varying degrees, although in some individuals one kind is more marked than the other, and sometimes first one kind and then the other dominates in the course of the same person's life.

In the love that has its source in the infant's experience there is essentially no element of status seeking, even though when it arises between adults it may confer a feeling of rank upon the giver. But in the other love, which arises out of the sexual drive, status seeking, competition, and therefore a certain aggressiveness, are intrinsic parts.

11

Preserving the Losers

The threads we have been following do not stand isolated; they intertwine with others to form the complex fabric of life. The influence of the individual filaments can only be appreciated if we look at them again, not separately, but as elements of the total design.

We have seen that in most higher animals a successful struggle for dominance culminates in a right to mate. (In some, of course, less dominant animals may also procreate, or at least become part of a reserve breeding pool, but dominance is always accompanied by mating privileges.) The contest for dominance sets the stage for breeding, and the struggle itself promotes the hormonal changes that equate high status with sexual activity, while the defeated animals experience inhibition of their sexual drive. They become largely asexual, with a potential for sexuality only in case the numbers of breeding animals are depleted, when they are available as replacements. The removal of a dominant animal from a group releases a subdominant one from its sexual inhibition.

A telling demonstration of this was observed by W. C. Dilger. He reported that if three African parrots (lovebirds) were put into a cage, two of them form a pair, and the one left out develops signs that suggest "depression." Its plumage becomes progressively rougher, patches appear, and it dies within six months. He noted that, in contrast, one lovebird left alone "does fine if not in the presence of an observable bond."

In this behavior we see that a contest of some kind must have taken place between two birds for the privilege of mating with the third. It could not have been a fight, or it would have been observed, and was surely a conventional contest on the basis of plumage or some other attribute. The winning bird gained the mate and thrived, but the losing bird, being confined in a cage and therefore denied the opportunity of entering any other contest, gave up and eliminated itself through a psychosomatic process. It was a loser, and nature's laws governing losers are rigid. The observation that a bird on its own did well demonstrates that it is the fact of losing that is lethal and not the caged condition.

Another worker, J. Price, was impressed (as have been so many ethologists) that macaques and baboons have especially well organized hierarchies and social arrangements in which *all* interactions between two or more animals are influenced by relative rank. He, too, noticed that when any change occurred in an animal's relative position, it showed changes in demeanor that he interpreted as elation when the animal was rising in rank and depression when its rank was lowered. (Obviously he could only speculate on the nature of the animal's moods, but the motor responses of these nonhuman primates are sufficiently close to our own to be recognizable.) Price, concerned with the evolution of mental illness, assumed that depression of this kind was adaptive in nature, since it prevented the descending animal from fighting back and thus disrupting the social order.

Throughout nature the fact of being a loser has very specific consequences. Nevertheless, the removal of a dominant animal from the presence of a loser enables the loser to regain the responses characteristic of dominance and makes it possible for it to enter into new contests. We cannot stress this factor strongly enough because it is at the core of successful treatment of inhibitions of sexuality in human beings.

One of the characteristics of our own species is that we consider it a virtue to succor the weak and to support and care for those who suffer any kind of disability. This impulse overflows from giving help to the weak of our own kind and prompts us to give aid to any creature that seems to be in need. We organize societies that find foster homes for stray animals and for preventing cruelty to them. A cat stuck between buildings prompts heroic measures to save it, and a child finding a bird with a broken leg or wing will carry it home, make a splint for it, and nurse it. Although we know perfectly well that an incapacitated wild animal stands no chance for survival when it is returned to its own group, we nevertheless feel impelled to assist one that is hurt or trapped. We avoid treading on a small creature if we can, although we are aware that its death will in no way affect its population, which will maintain a suitable number of individuals with or without this one. But we are human beings, programmed to give help, and much more so to our own kind. We have a caste of medical men to relieve bodily suffering, legal men to right social inequities, and scientists to improve the physical conditions of our lives. We honor ideals of service, self-sacrifice, and devotion to the welfare of the less fortunate. The result is that human losers are not eliminated but preserved and, moreover, considered to have as much right to mate as anyone else.

What do we mean by a loser? We do not necessarily mean a poor person, nor one who belongs to what are thought of as the lower ranks of society. There are dominant individuals among the poorest groups of human beings, just as there are losers among the wealthy. In every social group there are leaders, followers, and those who merely exist on the fringes. Leaders may be thought of as dominant animals and followers as the rank and file of the flock or herd, while those who exist on the fringes of any group—the hangers-on and also-rans—may be equated with the animal "losers" that are the first to be sacrificed, when necessary, by their societies.

It is necessary to stress this point, lest the reader object that poor people (apparently losers in the social sense) are often the most prolific breeders. We cannot emphasize enough that whether a person is a leader or a follower or a hanger-on is largely governed by the way he or she feels about himself or herself. A poor man may feel like a lord in his own home, while the son or daughter of an influential family may be scorned by his or her peers and feel less worthy than a beggar.

Dominance as it relates to status is not an absolute term. It is established according to the conventions of the social group in which the individual exists. In this contest each kind of social group must be thought of as a subspecies, with its own practices, aims, and ideals. Dominance, therefore, cannot be assessed in the terms of one culture and applied to another. It is at all times relative to the habits of the culture or subculture being observed, and it is often established by the inner strength of personality of an individual without regard to external value systems. The pride of a poor farmer who manages to support his family without getting into debt, the weakness and lack of self-esteem of the sons of great men, these are as much clichés of life as of fiction.

Among humans, "losers" on all levels, poor or rich, illiterate or educated, are not only permitted but expected to become breeding adults. However, the ancient mechanisms survive to some extent, with the consequence that sexual difficulties appear in many of those who feel subordinate.

These ancient mechanisms, acting as they do to enhance the sexuality of the dominant and to inhibit that of the subordinate, evolved in the service of the group as a whole. The individual was but an expendable unit in the totality of the group. One must have this in mind to understand how group standards and pressures work on the individual to give him a feeling about his place in it, high or low. Thus, in trying to find causes for sexual difficulties in our species, we often have to go beyond the range of an individual's experiences and seek to understand the values of the group in which that individual lives. Only our species systematically preserves its losers; the social expectations for marriage, home, and family exist in winner and loser alike.

Perhaps the best way to see how this works among human beings is to look at a family that affords a somewhat extreme example. The family we have in mind consists of a couple and their four sons. We are taking this particular family rather than one with sons and daughters, or with daughters only, because in our culture it is easier to assess the sexuality of a male than of a female, since we expect the male to take the initiative.

The father of this family has held a long series of low-paid jobs with periods of unemployment between them. He has been a metal spinner, a taxi driver, a cloakroom attendant, a waiter, a school janitor, and a post office auxiliary worker, with other short-lived jobs in between. The other men in his neighborhood held similar jobs, but they held them longer and made headway. His wife sometimes reproaches him, "Why do you quit? Joe has his own cab already and makes good money," or "Steve's become a foreman. Why couldn't you have held on longer? You'd have had the job."

In fact this man is neither lazy nor incompetent, and he has sufficient sense of responsibility to wish to provide for his family, but he has great difficulty in getting along with his fellow workers or with his bosses. Inevitably he is the butt of their humor or finds himself being picked on and feels tormented. Much of the teasing he experiences is probably no more than good-natured banter, but he over-reacts to it and feels slighted or "put down." Sometimes it is so painful to him that he is not able to face his fellow workers and doesn't show up on his job. Once or twice he has felt so cornered that he has attacked his "tormentors," but not being a fighter he was easily sub-dued each time and felt so annihilated that he has simply given up and not gone back to the job. It is significant that he has never been dismissed. He has always left of his own accord.

This man presents a perfect picture of a loser. In any other animal group he would have no way of surviving, but in our society he is supported by welfare funds, unemployment insurance, and, morally, the fact that he has a family depending on him for support drives him to efforts that he is not able to fulfill. Indeed in our well-meaning concern that all should be provided for, we force upon the non-dominant the burdens of family responsibilities. Unfortunately, our evolutionary heritage has endowed them with built-in reflexes that prevent them from carrying out this role—a fact that, given our codes of ethics, we do not and cannot accept.

In this particular family the mother, characteristically, is obliged to accept the roles of both mother and father and is of slightly stronger fiber, because she has to be. Without her the family would not survive. The sons look to her for guidance and regard their father much as they would another brother, as also dependent on their mother. She works when she can and contributes to the family income, which is occa-sionally also supplemented by small sums from her better-off bachelor brother-in-law. Under the pressure of her situation she not infre-quently makes disparaging comparisons between her husband and his more affluent brother.

The same spirit colors her relationship with her sons. When she feels pushed beyond her power to cope she sometimes explodes with, "I wish I'd had girls—they could help me. You boys are just as lazy as your no-good father." Nevertheless she has a soft spot for her oldest son, Leslie. From his earliest years he always tried to please her and took on tasks usually assigned to girls. When his mother worked he prepared the family's meals and did the marketing. The second son, Jimmy, has always been silent and withdrawn. As a child he opposed every request his mother made of him and often earned exasperated thrashings from her. Eddie, the third son, was rarely at home. When-ever he could he ran off to play, and he became a hanger-on of the local street gang. The youngest son, Henry, was the most harmed of all by the atmosphere of the home. The parents had hoped that Eddie would be their last child and made it clear that Henry was unwanted from the moment of his birth. As a result he was fearful, had no friends, and consistently failed at school. Indeed all the brothers had scholastic problems, and only the two oldest were able to complete high school.

The sexual history of these young men parallels their failures as social beings. Leslie never dated any girls. At the age of twenty-two he became involved in a homosexual "marriage" in which he suffered all kinds of indignities and abuse by his partner. Jimmy was twenty-five before he had his first girlfriend. She was a widow with a child, ten years his senior, inordinately obese and physically unattractive. He moved into her home but did not marry her. After a few futile attempts at a sexual relationship he never tried again. She constantly berated him on account of his sexual failure, and he countered with a silent rage. An occasional outburst, like the deliberate smashing of an ashtray, was the only indication of his inner fury. After several years this woman threw him out. It was a final indignity. Even this obese, unattractive, unwanted woman had no use for him. Since then Jimmy has spent his life in a hermitlike state, working only occasionally and living in an incredibly cluttered room from which he cannot bring himself to throw out anything. Newspapers that he has picked up from waste baskets over the years (for he buys nothing for himself but food) are stacked up almost to the ceiling.

The third son, Eddie, at the age of thirty married a girl of different racial origin. Now, after the first three years in which two children were produced, he has lost all sexual desire and has become a frequenter of neighborhood saloons.

Henry's social difficulties and psychological problems were so severe that he was kept back at school several times, and eventually, at the age of seventeen, he was referred by the school to a mental hygiene clinic. As part of a general study his entire background was investigated, and all the members of his family were interviewed. In this way we gained thorough knowledge of an entire nondominant family and the sexual history of their offspring. Henry expresses great fear of any kind of sexual involvement. He has recurrent nightmares involving genital injury. He sees women as threatening and frightening figures.

Such a family could hardly come into being in any other species, since the parents were the equivalent of what would have been peripheral animals in other groups and would not have mated. Even if they had, by some fortuitous circumstance, their offspring would not have had any chance of survival. All of them are clearly adaptive failures, and we can see nature's mechanisms powerfully influencing their lives in spite of human attempts to help them. As we can see, within two or three generations their genes will be eliminated from their group's breeding pool.

Admittedly this family presents an extreme example. In most instances we find less severe sexual difficulties based on social problems that are more difficult to identify. However, an awareness of the evolutionary social factors underlying sexual problems puts them into a context where it is possible to recognize also the milder forms and to deal with them with a chance for a satisfactory outcome.

There is another important point to be drawn from the example of this family. It is that different combinations of factors, all arising from the same setting, produce equally different varieties of sexual dysfunction. Today there is still a tendency in many medical and psychological circles to treat sexual difficulties as though they comprised an illness in themselves and not as symptoms of a wider disturbance of human functioning. In this family we saw four different kinds of sexual dysfunction arising from the same environment. Technically Leslie could be described as a passive, masochistic homosexual; Jimmy as withdrawn (schizoid) and incapable of feelings, including sexual ones; Eddie as having an avoidance mechanism against close involvement and preferring a "buddy" relationship to a sexual one, but without resorting to homosexual practices; Henry as suffering from sexual phobias. If these men sought help individually for their sexual difficulties, only their respective symptoms could be seen as entities in themselves. The specialists concerned would then deal with them separately. Valid as this approach is by today's thinking, its results are doomed to failure in the absence of the broader evolutionary concept of the significance of status. Without a radical readjustment of each brother's sense of his personal worth and value in his society (rank), no verbal, chemical, or surgical therapy is likely to prove helpful. Such individuals become the failures of therapy as they are of society.

Creating Losers

To get a perspective on human courtship, let us go back briefly to the courtship practices of most higher animals. Among them the female has various physical and behavioral means of making known that she is ready to be approached. When this is the case the more successful males, who have been identified by their own preliminary contests, approach her, and a mating is consummated. In some instances the mating is an isolated event, but in others a pair is formed at least for a season and sometimes even for the lifetimes of the animals concerned. This is true also in our own species, but our involvement in the conventions and practices that surround the pairing of two individuals masks the basic facts from us.

Each human group has its own feelings about what constitutes desirability in a young man or woman. In some the most esteemed attribute of a girl is beauty and of a boy strength or courage; in others intelligence is highly valued, or lineage, or wealth. There are groups in which a girl's domestic skills are prized above all else or a boy's hunting prowess; or her sturdiness and his manual skills. Whatever the desirable quality happens to be, there is always one that is recognized as worth striving for against others of the same sex in order to obtain the interest and affection of the person possessing it, and the degree to which that quality is possessed will determine the young person's rank in his or her social hierarchy.

This contest begins from earliest childhood. How often we hear a grandparent exclaim with pride and delight, "How pretty she is! She'll have all the boys running after her when she grows up," or, "He's so bright! There's no need to worry about his future." Right in the nursery a social hierarchy is being sorted out in exactly the same way that wrestling lion or wolf cubs sort out theirs and recognize their leaders by the time a generation reaches maturity.

From our own observation it seems to us that a young child who has very strong motivation and who determinedly pursues and masters the object of its interest without regard for whether the other children join him or her usually becomes a focus of the attention of the others. They gather round, want to know what the preoccupied one is doing, try to imitate, gravitate to other doers, and eventually become followers of one or the other of them. We have seen a three-year-old child consistently enter a nursery school room and make straight for the shelves that housed the most complicated building blocks. He would single-mindedly busy himself with these until he managed to erect quite impressive structures that caught the attention of the less motivated. These would then come over and ask him, "What are you making?" or announce, "I want to build too." They would attach themselves to him, copy him, and in a silent way acknowledge him as their master. Other children gravitated to a child who showed great initiative and daring in using gym apparatus, and this child too had his band of followers. In much the same way groups form themselves around highly motivated, innovative individuals in almost any walk of life among older children and also among adults. Of course, if a child has acquired an aura and a habit of leadership from earliest years that child is most likely to retain this quality as an adult, but this does not exclude the possibility (which we have all seen occur in some late bloomers) of a talent for or quality of leadership developing later.

Until about the time of the industrial revolution and what might be called the worldwide uniculture that is rapidly extending even to the last of the more isolated tribal peoples, certain recognized values formed the basis of rank in certain areas of the world. Among these were, for example, the warrior qualities that were essential for leadership in north European nations. Among Mediterranean peoples, however, the ability to produce or bear many children was a claim to approbation. Among Jews, traditionally, distinction was acquired by learning and intelligence, while in many tribal societies wealth in the form of herds or pots or other possessions was the route to respect. Today the traditional values are blurred, but the new ones emerging are just as varied. In industrial nations managerial and administrative abilities are highly esteemed, as are the special skills of people who achieve fame or notoriety through the news media, so that successful entertainers and athletes form a new aristocracy. But the social mechanism remains the same as it has always been: competition especially between males but also between females establishes a ranking order in each sex, so that those achieving high status are attractive to the ranking members of the opposite sex. The only feature that changes is the arena of the contest.

In modern urban centers the picture is clouded by the great diversity of ideals that coexist within them. In a group where girls knock themselves out over a football hero the scholar will not be valued, but in the same geographic area there may be another group that prizes the scholar's virtues; where the gang leader is king, the boy scout is despised, but where the good citizen is esteemed, the "bad boy" is the low man on the totem pole. In the more conservative societies of small towns, rural areas, and especially in tribal groups, values are more uniform and easier to discern.

Rank, then, plays its role in human groups. Among us, of course, individuals have alternatives that are not open to other animals, which must stand or fall by conventions established over eons of time and that change only extremely slowly. If a human being finds he cannot make the grade in one group, say where strength and daring are admired, he may be able to acquire status in another, where skills in art or music form the basis of social life.

Successful relationships depend basically upon mutual respect: a private acknowledgment by each partner of the rank of the other. Whatever quality established each partner's desirability above his or her peers during the social preliminaries to mating remains socially desirable and is the source of pride of each in the other that cements the bond. A man who married a woman because he found her beautiful will always be proud of her beauty, and she will be dear to him because of it even in old age when the merest traces of it remain. Another man may marry a woman because she is the daughter of a prestigious family and is very intelligent. All his life he will find opportunities to speak of her degrees and scholastic attainments and to mention her maiden name and the attainments of her family. He will continue to esteem her for those qualities that attracted him to her even if, to an outsider, she appears unattractive.

Rank involves expectations, in that the qualities that establish the status of a person become expected of him or her. Where rank is lost or diminished there is usually a falling away of those expected qualities, and this falling becomes a negative factor in the person's social relationships. Rank is equated with respect. Respect is based on the fulfillment of expectations. Failure to sustain expectations leads to loss of respect and eventually to sexual problems.

Failure to live up to expectations is one of the most outstanding elements in the disruption of any relationship. While in an animal group an individual that gains rank in early contests normally retains it throughout its mature life, in a human group circumstances may set a previously dominant person on to a downward path. Then, as a consequence of evolutionary mechanisms that are still with us, the sexuality that is part of the fabric of social organization becomes diminished, sometimes to the vanishing point, and in our culture this emerges as a medical problem and sexual disability.

12

Impotence and Frigidity

Only a few generations ago the parents and grandparents of those of us now in our middle years equated any aspect of sexuality with bathroom functions. No respectable person would raise either in polite company, and perhaps not privately. One woman relates that she was pregnant for four or five months without ever mentioning the fact to her mother-in-law, who would have considered it indelicate for her to have done so. Her mother-in-law learned of the impending arrival of a grandchild only when the fact was visibly incontrovertible. Another woman mentioned that she did not care to be seen outside her home in the last months of pregnancy and did not go out unless it was absolutely necessary. Her pregnancy made it clear that she must have been "subjected to the sexual attentions of her husband" (her terms), and it was considered extremely immodest to flaunt this fact in public. Our parents considered their sexual drives to be an imposition by nature on their better selves. Doors were locked. The unclothed human body was never seen.

In this atmosphere such sexual malfunctions as impotence and frigidity were masked. Frigidity could be covered under the cloak of chastity or virtue, and impotence behind a shield of morality or religious continence. Indeed, the conditions could be claimed as virtues. But today, those who suffer from these sexual disorders cannot hide them even from themselves. Ironically enough, sexual liberation has made impotence and frigidity more painful and incomprehensible than ever before to those who suffer from them.

In historic times there have been successive wavelike changes in sexual mores, from periods of repression to times of license. Rather than attempt to recount these, we are starting arbitrarily in the late Victorian era. This serves our purpose well because there are people alive today who have had personal experience of it and can express at firsthand how they felt, and also because the period from then until now has seen a full turn of the cycle from strong puritanical ways to the current anything-goes attitude.

It is, of course, impossible to back up our opinions about the sexual practices of other times with statistics. It is only very recently that any documentation has been attempted. It is intriguing to think what might have been the response to a question posed by a Kinsey interviewer to one of our parents or grandparents in their earlier years! Nevertheless, with the publication of some of the hidden writings of those times, and with the possibility of interviewing those still alive who had firsthand knowledge of the era (and who are more willing to speak now than they would have been then), we have the distinct impression that the proportions of highly sexual, moderately sexual, and sexually handicapped people have remained essentially the same over very long periods of time and are likely to continue to do so irrespective of the amount of freedom or lack of it that happens to be in vogue.

Handicapped sexuality having been an asset rather than a disadvantage in the cultural climate of late Victorian times, its existence might never have come to our notice had it not found expression through displacement into other bodily manifestations. Thus it came to the attention of Sigmund Freud in the form of hysteria. In prying open the world of sexuality to investigation he loosed what was at first a trickle but became a flood of theory about the significance of sexual experience in our lives and the causes and meaning of sexual difficulties.

Through self-observation and by studying patients who presented themselves in consulting rooms and hospitals, and influenced by the knowledge that was available to them, an increasing number of investigators then formulated a succession of ideas that seemed satisfactory and even all-encompassing to them and to their contemporaries, but that we now see as limited by their areas' specialty.

As understanding of evolution, genetics, animal behavior, and biology has increased alongside deeper knowledge of the workings of the mind and nervous system, a cross-fertilization has taken place, and bridges between all these sciences have become apparent. It is now possible to view man as a species among species, all subject to the same universal laws.

Each generation is inclined to lay the blame for sexual disorders at the door of the preceding one. Our parents, as well as some of the older members of our own generation, are inclined to blame the moral rigidity in which they were raised for their own difficulties. It is easy to foresee that our children will feel that their problems may be due to our overly permissive standards. In fact, we have just had a conversation with a close friend and her twenty-one-year-old son and were amused to hear him say to his mother, "I've always appreciated the freedom you've given me and the liberal views you've taken, but I'm not at all sure I'd take the same stand with my own children if I have any. I think I'd be afraid to. I feel just lucky it worked out well for me, but can you be lucky all the time?" And we have not infrequently heard similar views from other young adults.

In line with this we see at the moment a spate of articles, first in the medical press and now in popular magazines and newspapers, blaming the liberation of the modern woman for many of the modern man's sexual problems. The writers suggest that since women have been made aware of their right to sexual gratification, their expectation of top performance by their partners has become a source of trepidation that can be inhibiting to the male.

It seems clear that whichever generation one wishes to examine and whatever explanation happens to be offered currently, the one constant fact is that some proportion of each generation does not function effectively as procreators. What, then, actually is impotence or frigidity in man? Is it organic disease? Is it a psychological condition? Or is it a result of something that transcends both of these? When seen against the broad background of the evolution of life, and of man's place in this panorama, then startlingly, what we think of as a malfunction becomes clearly visible as an essential mechanism in nature's order.

In seeking understanding of this very puzzling phenomenon we must look for a satellite's-eye view of the whole vista in which it is one element. Although sexual disorder may be a malfunction in the life of an individual, we find that it has played an important part in the formation of social groups in all kinds of animals. Moreover, viewing it in this way can be a valuable aid in alleviating the difficulties of the individual.

Discounting the occasions when sexual disorder is a byproduct of such debilitating diseases as diabetes or tuberculosis or of diseases directly affecting the organs of reproduction like tumors and venereal diseases, we find that in general impotence and frigidity have nothing to do with the sex organs. Psychologists believe they have found the clue in the character makeup of the individual. But we find that this does not go far enough. Psychology is only one link in a much longer chain.

If the individual is regarded as an entity, without considering his relations with the social groups of which he is a part, the cause of sexual malfunction is not apparent. Indeed it cannot be, because it does not reside in the individual organism. When we regard the individual as a part of his group, a new element emerges: his relative standing in it. Here we come to the crux of the matter: *status*. Men and women, as well as other animals, exist on more than one level: as individuals and as units of a larger group. These groups, too, function as parts of populations and of species, but that is not our subject here.

The workings of the group do not always favor the workings of its members. On the contrary, the needs of the group override the needs of the individual in all species. Man is the only animal that attempts to put the demands of the individual first, but the ancient mechanisms remain.

The inextricably close connection between a feeling of status and an ability for copulatory performance becomes ever clearer as we delve into the sources of impotence and frigidity.

By now we have seen the remarkably efficient mechanism by which an interbreeding group of animals keeps its population density in consonance with the capacity of its environment to support it. Since this normally limits a group's numbers to below the individuals' power to reproduce, competition is automatically set up in each generation and in higher animals takes conventional forms.

It is as if a habitat were a theater with a limited number of seats, into which entrance is not offered on a first-come-first-served basis. To enter this theater there is a preliminary contest, played by highly specific rules. In this way the theater is never crowded, and each ticket-holder is assured of comfortable space. As an added bonus, because of the preliminary weeding out, the members of the audience are those best able to make use of what the theater has to offer. As for those that fail to gain entrance, some stay around in case a place should become available, others give up and go away.

To make such a scheme workable in life, the biological apparatus of the participants has to be attuned so that each accepts his lot. The individual who gains a place in the theater must be one who will perform the task of perpetuating life's processes. The individual left outside must in some way lose his drive to enter.

This adaptive mechanism has proved to be the most efficient in the perpetuation of life and, as a result, it is almost universal. And since competition exists among social groups just as it does among individuals, automatically the most efficiently organized groups persist while others fall away. Nature's proverbial parsimony is an instrument in this overall picture. When any organ is not used, either because there is no longer need for it or because its use is prevented, its ability to function diminishes, and sometimes the organ itself eventually becomes vestigial. One has only to look at a limb after a cast is removed. After even a short time it is surprising how much the muscles have shrunk.

The same is true when there is no longer use for a drive. The glands that promote it cease functioning or at any rate cease switching on that particular drive. Thus an animal that has lost in competition painlessly becomes asexual, at least temporarily, for nature's parsimony does not go so far as to eliminate prudence. The temporarily asexual animals form a reserve that can be drawn on when need arises.

Similar mechanisms existed in groups of hunting man and still exist in those few corners of the earth where tribal life is undisturbed. In most cases the peoples concerned are probably unaware of the effects of their customs in promoting population stability. It is a remarkable fact that populations of tribal groups have remained approximately the same through millennia, without any deliberate planning or the scientific means to effect such plans, had they been made. Early human groups inherited practices from their past as part of the animal world at large, and tribal societies codified these practices into custom. The human population explosion did not begin until technical competence led man to believe that he can always increase his food supply according to the needs of his numbers and that he no longer must adjust his numbers to his resources. Whether this turns out to be true in the long run remains to be seen, but in the meantime it has resulted in medical arts that keep alive children who in the past would not have been saved and the idea that every individual has the right, indeed in the church view the duty, to reproduce. This is yet another instance where man's reasoning brain contravenes the natural processes established by eons of evolution in his other bodily organs and functions. In this case it has produced an area of contention between mind and body that for many people is a source of deep distress.

The more primitive brain of other animals, and the core of the primitive brain that remains within our own, automatically switches off sexual drive when it is superfluous to the group's needs. Man's newer, reasoning brain does not accept this automatic inhibition and seeks ways to circumvent it. In this dichotomy emotional pain arises in us that cannot arise in the animal whose brain's instructions are direct and unequivocal.

What, today, is the actual experience of a victim of impotence who has no idea whatever of the forces operating in him? In extreme instances he has profound feelings of shame and despair. One expressed it, "I wish I could go to bed in the evening and not wake up. Life has no interest for me anymore." His distress deepens because he feels he cannot discuss the matter even with professionals who might be able to help him, for he fears their ridicule as much as the rest of society's. Some feel intense anger toward themselves, as if they were responsible for their condition. "What kind of man am I?" such a person may exclaim, or "I'm only half a man!" Sometimes these feelings take form in self-destructive tendencies, like reckless driving at high speed.

Such reactions by no means exhaust the repertoire of responses to the pain of shame. There are some who attempt to dull it by resorting to alcohol or to drugs, some who retire into lethargy and find it difficult or impossible to get up in the mornings or to get out of bed at all. Naturally these courses represent extremes of reaction. Many degrees and variations of these tendencies exist, but underlying them all is a sense of self-worthlessness, of the meaninglessness of their existences, and a desire, conscious or unconscious, to remove themselves from the ranks of their societies.

In this basic desire there is a continuation of the mechanisms that operate in all animal groups. The defeated animal relinquishes its drive for dominant status, accepts defeat, and removes itself from the central arena of the group's life and from its pool of breeders. It becomes a peripheral creature, available to participate only if a place is made for it by the removal of a dominant one, but more usually it becomes a sacrifice to predators, a victim of parasites or disease or of death from the shock of its defeat.

The mechanism just described applies most precisely to herd animals or to species where social groups are strongly cohesive. But there are countless forms of social organization, and in many species the results of failure are not quite so dire. The social structure of our close primate relatives the chimpanzees, for instance, is not so closely knit as that of herd animals. Among them the dominant animal has precedence in mating, but the subordinate is not entirely excluded. However, in the presence of a higher-ranking animal the lower-ranking one is sexually inhibited, and he waits. Adolescent chimpanzee males are inhibited by the presence *of any* adult male.

This behavior is quite suggestive in our self-understanding, for here we have in a closely allied species a temporary blocking of the sex drive that is not permanently disabling. The response comes very close to what we call temporary impotence in human beings.

Thus we can recognize in impotence not disease but an essential social mechanism that exists throughout nature and serves to enhance a group's power to survive by reserving the right and the ability to breed to the best-adapted, dominant few. In this light it is less surprising that human impotence has rarely yielded to treatment by drugs or the various experimental transplant operations. Psychological insight therapy and counseling have had a better record, but for many individuals they too have fallen short. However, if we bring understanding gained from the field of evolutionary anthropology to the fields of psychology and medicine, we find a new dimension.

The treatment of impotence has been, and to a large extent still is, an attempt to deal with what is in effect the last link in a long chain of events. Whether they offered incantations, aphrodisiacs, or drugs, medical men from the tribal shaman to the modern M.D. have seen impotence as a disease or disability of the sex organs only. In our times, even before the synthesis of testosterone was achieved, some doctors attempted to find a biological remedy and administered an extract of bull's or monkey's testicles.

There is no question but that administering testosterone works well with other animals, as has been amply demonstrated in primate centers. In man, however, psychological effects play so much greater a role that they diminish or nullify the power of testosterone to enhance feelings of status. For this reason the artificial administration of testosterone has no place as a "cure" for impotence in man.

And what of frigidity? Because of our cultural expectation that a female should be less aggressive in sexual behavior, and also because her anatomy makes it easier for her to mask feelings of sexual inadequacy, frigidity is usually less anxiety-provoking to a woman than is impotence to a man. When a woman is subjected to stress, it is usually not of frigidity that she complains. She will tell her doctor that she "always feels tired," that she "can hardly drag herself around," that her work is not appreciated, that her children and her husband make too many demands on her. In fact, she is depressed. She may participate in sexual activity, but she does not enjoy it. She considers it to be either a nuisance or just another imposition by her husband. It is rare that she herself complains that anything is wrong with her sexually. Usually it is her husband who brings up the subject.

The element that emerges most strikingly from women who suffer from depression is their almost total inability to assert themselves, a bane that usually clouds their entire lives. They provide the most glaring examples of lack of status. (We are not speaking here, of course, of the depression that is a consequence of the loss of a loved person or possession.) At home, the personality of the depressed woman is rather unattractive. Nothing pleases her. She moans and complains and feels victimized by everyone. Any responsibility seems overwhelming to her, but whenever she is asked to take on a task she is unable to refuse. She is in constant need of approval and is afraid that if she disagrees with an opinion or refuses a request she will lose affection. But this is not the picture that these women present publicly. In their quiet way they make attempts to please, but they are often unsuccessful and have difficulties with neighbors and friends as well as with their own families. The sexual problem that results from this kind of depression is diminished interest. Their tendency to submit, and then to resent their submission, infiltrates their sexual relationship.

Some doctors have wondered why the patient who is so irritable at home is so docile and anxious to please her physician. Indeed, comments on this have appeared in papers in the medical literature. We would suggest that the status of the doctor is so undisputed in her mind that she makes no attempt to compete with him, but with her husband and family her plaints represent her generally futile attempts

at self-assertion that intensify her complaints. It is especially note-
worthy that if a doctor becomes overly friendly with this kind of
patient, she then gives him the same hard time that she metes out to
her family.

In the absence of any feeling of status, the attitudes of women
invite further rejection. They are peripheral individuals. They have no
appetite, they can't sleep, they have no energy—all their functions are
diminished. They are inadequate socially, personally, and, not the
least, sexually. Any attempt to deal with the sexual factor in isolation
can only increase their sense of futility and aggravate their problem,
which is their absence of rank.

Flashback: The Background

In 1135 Maimonides wrote, "Coitus does much harm to many
people ... the essential organs will dry up and become cold. ...
Coitus harms all the members in general, its harm to the brain is more
so." For a caliph's waning sexual vigor, he recommended "eating of
borax and mustard grain ... take a little of cubebs, pyrethrum, ginger,
and cinnamon. ... From that moment she will have such an affection
for you that she can scarcely be a moment without you. The virile
member rubbed with ass's milk will become uncommonly strong and
vigorous. Green peas, boiled with onions, and powdered cinnamon,
ginger, and cardamons, well pounded, create for the consumer considerable amorous passion and strength for the coitus."

As late as 1848, Sir Alfred Morrison wrote, "It is well known that
the abuse of coition enervates the whole frame and in particular
enfeebles the functions of the brain bringing on hypochondriasis,
insanity, and epilepsy."

As the concept of disease has advanced from a magical basis to a
disturbance of bodily humors and finally to an understanding of its
basis in many causes, it has been subjected to a continuing revision of
classifications, and a parallel change in the kind of expert—from witch
doctor to priest to leech to barber to doctor—who dealt with it.

Until very recently, and even today in most parts of the world,
sexual problems are considered the domain of the general practitioner, or at best of the specialist in genitourinary diseases. Sexual
disorders are not even dignified as problems worthy of a separate
specialty, but are lumped together with problems arising from the
functions of the excretory organs merely because of their proximity!

There is no question but that in a very limited number of cases local disease, like an inflamed prostate gland, or a debilitating condition like tuberculosis may cause impotence and require the services of these doctors. But by far the largest number of cases involving impotence do not fall within their spheres of competence.

Characteristically, when medications (hormone injections, tonics, pep pills, tranquilizers, and the like) have failed, these doctors fall back upon what one can only call locker-room advice, crude and explicit: Get yourself an experienced woman who knows how to treat you. The implication is that there is nothing wrong with the impotent man and that his wife is at fault for not knowing how to arouse him. Frequently these men are dismayed by this lack of seriousness about what, to them, is a very distressing condition.

A woman with sexual difficulties has it a little easier. First of all, it is only quite recently that she is likely to have realized that she had a problem at all, since she was reared to consider herself the passive object of the act and not a participant in it. More recently, if her husband found her unresponsive, he might have sent her to a doctor to check whether an organic impediment existed, in which case she came as the bearer of a message from her husband and not as a complainant. In those cases the doctor usually reassured her that there was nothing wrong with her, gave her some pills, and advised her at least to pretend to be interested in her husband's advances.

It is really only today that most women expect sexual pleasure and have either blamed their husbands, turned to other men, or sought professional help if they have not received it. Now the woman has joined the man in developing anxieties about sexual performance, especially if her experience does not meet her expectations of what is attainable.

A slightly more encompassing view has been taken by those who follow Pavlov's ideas that all behavior, including sexual, is a learning process acquired by conditioning. For them, sexual difficulties arise from faulty conditioning, and their remedy is to attempt to rectify the incorrect learning. They do this by means very similar to those Pavlov used in getting his dogs to salivate at the sound of a bell. By accustoming the patient to some painful association (like an electric shock) with behavior that is undesirable (like homosexuality) and by reinforcing with a pleasurable experience the behavior that is considered desirable, they aim to set up automatic reflexes that program the individual to act in what they consider to be an acceptable way. In treating impotence they attempt to decondition the anxieties surrounding sex. It is easy to see that their results cannot be more impressive than those of the purely medical approach, because the behaviorist, like the medical man, is dealing only with the symptom. This approach is like trying to repair a damaged submarine by rearranging the periscope, the only part of it that can be seen above water.

In discovering that there is indeed a submarine below the periscope—or, as he put it, an iceberg of which only a small fraction is visible—Freud opened the way to a more radical understanding of human response. Postulating that all pleasure is ultimately sexual (libidinal theory), he suggested that the grounds for all adult responses are laid in early childhood and especially in the period of maternal handling with its attendant satisfactions.

Freud considered these first pleasurable sensations sexual in essence and an individual's first sexual experience—an idea that has met many objections. It seems to us that this is a linguistic problem rather than a biological one: if one defines all pleasure as being in some way sexual, these early physical pleasures must be called sexual. But if we reserve the word *sexual* for genital activity leading to mating, clearly the child's experience does not fall into this category. In all fairness, since life is a continuum and what happens in infancy and childhood paves the way for what happens later, one must acknowledge that there was some validity in Freud's point of view. We see puppies and cubs mounting each other in a playful way that is entirely asexual, but nevertheless that pattern will develop sexual content as the animals mature. In most tribal societies of man this type of "sexual" activity in children was accepted indulgently, and no taboo was associated with it. Only when the children reached puberty and the behavior became truly sexual were the regulatory taboos invoked.

Freud also stressed that beyond the pleasure the young male felt via his genital apparatus was the very great sense of pride he felt in it, a pride that the young female was unable to feel. Deprived of it, he argued, she was bound to experience what he termed penis envy.

There is no question but that most ideas, however original or inspired, are influenced by the cultural climate of their times. As we all know, Freud lived toward the end of an epoch in which the role of the female was on the one hand so played down that she was considered almost a lower order of creature, and on the other so idealized that she was hardly of flesh and blood, much less a sexual creature, in the minds of most males.

When any activity, drive, or function is suppressed by social dictum, the brain reacts by occupying itself unduly with it. If we tell a child that she may not open a certain door, she will spend her days wondering what lies behind that door, imagining the most fanciful creatures or the most lurid scenes. She will try to discover why she may not open the door, she will touch the door and turn its handle, and she will think of many totally extraneous things in terms of that door. To give a concrete example of this tendency, when prohibition was the law in the United States almost every adult person spent time and energy pursuing trails that led to alcohol and thoughts of getting a drink occupied more minds than they ever have before or since. In Freud's day sex was the suppressed function, hidden behind veils of secrecy and inhibition. Because of this there was without doubt undue subconscious concern with sex, and it seemed to Freud that this provided a key to areas of human behavior that were not fully understood. It was therefore quite natural that Freud should have found sexual explanations for the problems he sought to solve, and that in his own time, given the excessive preoccupation with what went on behind the door closed on sex, these explanations were accepted as (and in many cases were) valid. There have been quite a few female patients, extensively described in psychiatric literature, whose fantasies lent themselves to the penis-envy interpretation. And we cannot overlook the practices of some lesbians who assume the male role. But these are extremes of human behavior, and one cannot generalize from them as though they were an indication of the norm.

When Freud originated the idea of penis envy, it was difficult if not impossible for most women to accept it. To a woman busy in her household and fulfilled by her maternal role, the idea of envying this organ of male anatomy appeared nonsense. It was only later, when the female emerged from the household and began to enter what had previously been all-male realms of business and the professions, that the theory of penis envy began to have some relevance, and then only as a purely symbolic representation of envy of the male role, not of his anatomy.

In Freud's time, and to a large extent today, most people believed that there was a fundamental difference between a woman's brain and thought processes and those of a man. A man was considered to be capable of mathematical calculation, logical thinking, and abstract conceptions that were beyond the mental powers of females. On the other hand, refined sensibilities and powers of intuition were attributed to women. When a few intelligent women had the courage to break out of the roles assigned them and gave evidence of high intellectual qualities, they were patronizingly told that they had "a man's head on their shoulders." In this area, in fact, it could indeed be said that there existed female envy of the male. Knowing her own capacity for logical thought (even if belittled as "common sense") and aware of her own mental powers, she must indeed have revolted inwardly when obliged to play the vapid, superficial, "delicate" part assigned to her. Freud would probably have been closer to the mark had he named the feelings he was trying to identify "role envy" rather than penis envy.

Ibsen was far ahead of Freud in his understanding of female psychology and of the revolt that must inevitably arise from the unnatural subjugation of women of the time. His play based on this theme, *A Doll's House*, is so to the point that it seems almost uncannily contemporary to us when played today.

Another logical outcome of Freud's view of infantile pleasure as sexual in essence was his contention that the growing boy competes with his father for the love of his mother, the so-called Oedipus Complex. He based this theory on many observations that can easily be corroborated by anyone who has daily contact with a developing child. A little boy feels that his mother belongs to him and sometimes resents the intrusion of his father. But to this we have to add that he may sometimes feel possessive of the company of his father too and tell his mother to go away. From a biological point of view one could easily explain this with the dependency of the child on his mother and his absolute need of her protective presence (or his father's, if the father happens to be in focus). When a little boy announces, as sooner or later most of them do, "When I grow up I'm going to marry mummy," all he may be expressing is his desire to keep her looking after him. One could find corroboration of this thesis in the fact that many men do just that: marry women like their mothers, who continue to look after them!

If one looks back into childhood and tries to remember one's most devastating emotional experience, the terror of feeling lost, of not being able to find one's way back home, of being abandoned by one's parent (or parent substitute), far outweighs any other. The observed fact that a little boy is made unhappy by the idea of his father taking his mother away can also find its place in this context, and it is not necessarily to be interpreted as sexual jealousy.

Freud concluded that as a result of his competition with his father for his mother the small boy would be afraid of being punished by his father with castration. To him this explained some of the deep-seated anxieties manifested by many adult patients. But it seems to us that many of these anxieties, present as they are in an insecure individual, relate to his fear that satisfaction of his inordinate dependency needs may be cut off—in fact, that it is abandonment by the care-giving woman that threatens his security rather than memories of an infantile fear of castration by his father.

An extension of this is to be found in the modern indictment of the bossy female as a "castrator." As we see it, by putting a man down such a woman is lowering his rank in his own eyes and in the eyes of the world, with the effect of reducing his ability to function sexually. What the man reacts to is the attack on his self-esteem. The consequence on his sexual function is secondary. It can happen, as it often the case, that at a later date in describing his difficulties to his doctor he may mention his impotence, the secondary factor. The primary factor, his reduced sense of status, will not be mentioned because he is too ashamed to admit this.

Freud, sparked by the then very new understanding of evolution, tried to place his ideas about the Oedipus Complex and castration anxiety into an evolutionary context. He envisaged that in earliest times men had lived in a "primal horde" in which fathers and sons competed with each other until the sons slew the fathers and took possession of their sisters and mothers. He believed that it was to prevent a recurrence of such an event that incest taboos became culturally embedded. He did not take into account, because in his time the information was not available, that mechanisms tending to obviate incest are older than man, and that incest taboos are a cultural expression of a biological propensity. As in other primates the dominance of the mother inhibits the son from sexual behavior toward her, so also in earliest man must similar mechanisms have existed—mechanisms that eventually became enshrined in cultural practice.

Some of Freud's disciples felt that his ideas about the prominence of sex in human personality development were too narrow, and they broke away, forming a new school of thought. These men believed that the development of a person's character is solely dependent on cultural influences, that is, on the way he is brought up and on the standards of the society he is raised in. They went further and suggested that this had a circular effect, that the culture itself is determined by the way the infants are reared. Orthodox Freudians referred to them somewhat deprecatingly as "Culturalists" and accused them of focusing too narrowly on the differences that exist among various cultures in handling infants and raising children. Some of them did indeed become "armchair anthropologists" and incidentally sparked a totally new trend in anthropology. Until then anthropologists had studied only the customs and rites of groups as they found them and had not concerned themselves with their child-rearing practices. Prompted by the ideas of the Culturalists, anthropologists discovered a whole new and fertile field of study.

Geza Roheim occupied a place between the two extremes. For Freudians the child was a little monster, possessing untamed drives that had to be socialized. Perhaps in this attitude they were somewhat influenced by the Victorian view of the child as more or less a nuisance that should be kept out of the way until it was sufficiently grown up to be fit to associate with, for in Freud's time Victorian nannies were instructing their charges that "children should be seen and not heard." Shaw summed up the prevailing attitude when he referred to them as incomplete adults that leaked at both ends.

Roheim placed less emphasis on the Oedipus Complex as such and more on the helplessness of the infant. One could look at his views as an expression of the changing attitudes that resulted in the complete revolution in the treatment of children that has taken place from Victorian aloofness to our current child-centeredness. Roheim said that because the brain developed in the period of close relationship of the child to the mother, the personality development of the child had to be influenced by its dependence on her and that its developing ability to feel affection was centered on her for this reason.

A long step further in the same direction was taken by Alfred Adler. It seemed to him that the infant must feel like a helpless creature surrounded by giants, and later, when he is a grown man, he still feels helpless against the forces of nature. Even today so many of us are born and raised in cities where we are hardly aware of the forces of nature, but severe storms, tidal waves, floods, earthquakes, and landslides still remind us that we are comparatively powerless.

Adler's ideas about the child's feelings of helplessness are borne out in nursery stories of giants and ogres that the imagination of man has conjured up all through the ages. For Adler it was our helplessness rather than our sex drive that provided the clue to the development of individual personality. He believed that we all strive to overcome this sense of inferiority, and that sometimes in doing so we overshoot the mark and reach for superiority, power, and mastery over nature. Many of Adler's ideas have been crystallized into the terms "inferiority complex," "superiority complex," "power drive," "overcompensation," now so much part of our language we no longer remember their origin.

Still later in modern times Karen Horney, traveling the same road as Adler, saw the child and the adult not only as helpless but also as isolated in a hostile world and forever striving for security. Out of her thoughts came the current concepts of the importance of self-esteem and ideas about alienation and anomie in modern life.

It is interesting to see that about a century of psychological theory has either led or closely paralleled changing cultural patterns—from Freud's view of the child as "a being that loves itself with a supreme egotism" (primary narcissism), along the paths and way stations of his many followers, to Adler's and Horney's views of the child as helpless and isolated. Needless to say, when people with sexual problems turned to psychological theorists for help, this progression of ideas influenced the kind of treatment they were offered.

That so many variations and departures from the original theory have arisen is only accounted for by the fact that while all of them had much to offer, none of them alone was entirely satisfactory. The search for an all-encompassing principle is still continuing, but meanwhile a pragmatic tendency has appeared to turn again to the direct approach in the treatment of sexual dysfunction. The difference between the new trend and that of the behaviorists is that the latter attempted to recondition the individual from what was believed to be a purely personal disturbance, whereas the latest method, as practiced notably by Masters and Johnson, treats a couple together as an interacting unit. Here, too, we can see scientific practice largely influenced by the prevailing cultural atmosphere. In the climate of sexual equality of our time it would be almost impossible to conceive of either the male or the female alone as being solely "at fault."

All these approaches (except the last one) were, of course, endeavors to understand the total human personality and (Freud notwithstanding) not just sexual function. But if we return to the evolutionary point of view and see the roots of sexual impediment in the structure of life itself, we can bring new interpretations to each school of thought.

The administration of hormones to a person who is not hormone-deficient does not work in man, whose brain and its learning processes can influence his sexuality in complex ways. A man we have known for the greater part of his life (he is now in his early fifties) provides an illustration of this.

He was the son of an extraordinarily successful banker and younger by some fifteen years than his sister. His father had very little time for him, and he was left very much to the care of his nurse and his mother, who coddled and overprotected him. As a result, by the time he was about eighteen his manner was a trifle effeminate. He had not the slightest suggestion of homosexuality, but his mannerisms were not very manly. His voice was rather high-pitched, he giggled when he felt unsure of himself; moreover, he was blond and good-looking in what was thought of as a rather unmasculine way. This troubled his father, who sent him for medical treatment. He was dosed with large quantities of hormones. As a result he grew a coconut matting of dark hair on his chest, back, and limbs (although on the crown of his head he became bald early), but his slightly effeminate manner persisted; obviously it had to, since it was simply an expression of his training.

Dr. Alan J. Cooper has cogently summarized the complexity of the role of testosterone in health and disease. The data that apparently support a significant functional role for testosterone are:

1. There is a significant reduction in urinary testosterone levels in impotent men (compared with levels in matched controls), presumably reflecting reduced synthesis.

2. Some impotent men with markedly reduced testosterone levels fail to respond with urinary testosterone elevation to human chorionic gonadotrophin (HCG) stimulation, suggesting impaired synthesis.

3. Reduction or complete loss of potency has been noted following antiandrogenic treatment with cyproterone acetate, with a concomitant reduction in plasma testosterone (both effects are reversible when drug treatment is stopped).

4. There is a clinical improvement, with a slight reduction in pathologically elevated plasma testosterone levels, when antiandrogenic cyproterone acetate is given in cases of precocious puberty.

5. Plasma testosterone is elevated following coitus and during rapid eye movement (REM) sleep, when erections and seminal emissions are known to occur.

Data that seem to deny an important functional role for testosterone in impotence are:

1. Generally poor therapeutic response to methyltestosterone, various testosterone esters, and "testosterone aphrodisiac mixtures," with newer synthetic androgens such as mesterolone, even when recipients' urinary and plasma testosterone levels are markedly reduced.

2. Failure to produce clinical improvement in chronically impotent men with clomiphene, despite the drug's effect of doubling testosterone levels to above "normal."

3. Observation that male homosexuals who are highly active and potent may nevertheless have urine and plasma levels of testosterone much lower than "normal."

We agree with Dr. Cooper's view that testosterone has a subordinate feedback role in facilitating arousal and response, but that it plays a more important role in sustaining aggression and fertility. The reduction of testosterone in the systems of the chronically impotent and in the old-age group is probably a reflection of sexual apathy rather than a cause of it.

The behaviorists, instead of trying to increase the individual's hormone level, attempted to correct his behavior by setting up a new set of conditioned reflexes. Where the behaviorists had successes they believed their methods validated, but a closer look reveals that results were usually due to the personalities of certain doctors, who were able to imbue their patients with a feeling of confidence. Doctors who were unable to convey this sense of confidence usually had less success.

The ability to inspire confidence played no small role in the results of the Freudians and post-Freudians, regardless of the school of thought they followed. The insights gained through their explanations were undoubtedly helpful to some of their patients in improving their sexual as well as their general social functioning, but unless the insights were accompanied by a feeling of improvement in status, sexual problems (especially impotence or frigidity) usually remained unchanged.

In Adler and Horney, however, we find precursors of our own views. Adler brought into focus two essential characteristics of man: his infantile helplessness and his drive for power. Observing the important part each played, he felt there was a connection between them. It is here that we part company with him, for while we agree that infantile helplessness is of the essence in man's development, we see the drive for power as a completely separate endowment, arising out of the evolutionary necessities of a breeding group that can survive only by perpetuating its best stock. What Adler saw as a person's power drive (individual psychology) and unrelated to the social group as a whole, we see as participation in conventional competition, an inevitable and basic element of the life of an interbreeding group.

Adler must have had some inkling of the true nature of the "power drive" as a *social* force, because he commented at some length on an unbridled drive for power as a pathological condition. For us this is more simply seen as deviant behavior where a natural mechanism becomes misused. The criminal, bandit, or dictator is not confining his drive within the accepted rules of social competition, but is asserting naked aggression unbounded by convention.

This theory is borne out in our ideas about fair play. Competing animals all possess the same basic equipment, and the best or strongest emerges. When two humans, equally armed, fight a duel, we can discover who is the best swordsman or who is the fastest on the draw. In the early romantic movies this was well understood: Douglas Fairbanks or Errol Flynn tossed a sword back to his disarmed adversary. To have killed an unarmed opponent would have been felt as cowardly, not manly. About the same difference exists between natural social competition and unbridled aggression. To serve any useful end the contest must be on equal terms. To see how very basic this is we have only to listen to children, who have a very strong sense of fair play.

Karen Horney, as well as Adler, was concerned primarily with the individual, but her views dovetail perfectly with our view of the individual as a unit of a larger whole. Her stress on the search for security and the individual's sense of isolation underlines the two levels of our existence: for ourselves alone and at the same time as part of our society. She stresses interaction between people and the human being's feeling that his life only has meaning for him when he is part of a group. A person who feels separated from all groups has the feeling that nothing he does is of any consequence, and this leads to a sense of his own futility.

It is easy to see that Adler and his followers view any sexual problem as a consequence of a feeling of inferiority, and that Horney and hers see it as one of insecurity, and that both their views can be seen as different facets of a larger picture.

Now yet another new approach is taking its place alongside the older ones. Today's social egalitarianism, together with the scientific raising of children and the inordinate amount of attention devoted to them, is carried over into the treatment of sexual difficulty as practiced by Masters and Johnson and their followers. They view sexual difficulties purely pragmatically, as did the behaviorists, but they differ from them in asserting that problems can only be remedied by active cooperation between two people and not by one of them alone. In keeping with the ideas of our times, they give much attention to proper techniques with a goal of adequate functioning, but unlike the purveyors of some sex manuals they do not extol the sexual gymnast as the ideal.

The Masters and Johnson method has produced considerable success, and we believe it has a great deal of merit. However, we also believe that the reasons for their success go beyond the apparent ones. The obvious advantages of their method lie in the fact that both partners are able to discuss openly what has been a private torment. To a man or woman raised in an atmosphere in which discussion of sexual matters is difficult, this openness is already an enormous advantage. They are relieved of a great deal of the shame they feel in their inadequacy. Solving the sexual problem becomes a project on which the couple can work together and not an unmentionable thing that separates them. But from our point of view the overriding element in all of this is that the patients in such an institute become objects of the attention, interest, and concern of doctors, nurses, attendants, and technicians. They are treated as important, and this sense of their importance helps in raising them in their own esteem. Compare this with the jocular and somewhat demeaning advice of the old-fashioned general practitioner mentioned earlier and one can see the reason for the difference in the patients' response. A feeling of status restored instead of status lowered plays a large part in the relief of their symptoms.

We view the problem of impotence or frigidity as a social one that must be seen in its larger context to be handled successfully. Whether it should be treated at all is a philosophical question. We could suggest that it is in the interest of the society that its members' reproductive potential is partly controlled by natural means. But if we take the view that an individual's personal pain should be alleviated, then the most effective way to do so is to attempt to restore his feeling of self-worth. Once a human being's confidence in his personal value is restored, the biological problem of impotence in all likelihood will disappear.

13

Mind Over Sex

In trying to understand the close connection between sex and status in all of nature, we cannot overlook that other factor in man that can complicate or enhance everything we do and are. This additional factor is the human mind, or at least some of its higher functions, especially imagination, fantasy, and judgment.

Imagination

Imagination is called upon when a thing desired is not immediately obtainable or a wish is not yet fulfilled. Whn we feel the first rumblings of hunger our thoughts turn toward food; not only to getting or preparing it, but also to a vision of the eventual appetizing meal. This may be a trivial observation, but it refers to a phenomenon, however unremarkable, that has its place in life's processes. Thoughts promote alleviating action, and the mind prepares the body for the action that is to come.

For example, when an athlete crouches at the starting line prepared to spring into action, his heart rate increases *before* the sound of the starter's pistol. In such circumstances imagination is a facilitating mechanism. It serves the same function in our sex life. The anticipation of a sexual exchange sets into motion glandular secretions that will facilitate intercourse when and if it occurs. If external circumstances interfere with the completion of the anticipated event, both imagination and the mechanisms it sets into motion subside. If the time of the meal is postponed, our anticipatory salivation wanes; if the starter's pistol fails to go off, the athlete's heartbeat returns to normal. The same ebbing occurs if any other physical mechanism is aroused unduly. We may feel a temporary sense of discomfort or irritation, but that is all.

In our sex life, however, imagination plays a wider part than the simple triggering of glandular secretions. It is largely through imagination that we are able to transmute this purely physical drive into the emotion we call love. We are going to be talking more about love in our next chapter, but we cannot write of imagination and sex without a reminder of the power of the mind to promote bodily responses through imagination.

As beauty resides in the eye of the beholder, so our idealization of sex into romance and love largely resides in the imagination of the lover. His aroused emotions heighten and intensify his perceptions. The flowers he sees are prettier and their perfumes more intoxicating; every detail on the landscape stands out and is etched in his memory. He sees things he never noticed before. A young woman is not the most beautiful on earth for everybody; she only appears to be so in the mind of the young man who is in love with her. Neither is any man the handsomest or the noblest by any absolute standard, but he may seem to be so in some woman's imagination. The imagination is an instrument that raises the status of the love-object, and in doing so it performs a very important function in mating. After all, as we have seen, in many higher animals it is chiefly or only the high in rank that mate. It may seem prosaic to see love as a purely biological prelude, and not as the ideal our poets have made of it, but who can say that other animals do not have some equivalent feelings when they are attracted to their mates?

We do not really know what motivates other animals. Our ethologists hesitate to use the word *emotions* when describing their behavior for fear of anthropomorphizing. They speak of an animal's "programmed responses" as being triggered by certain signals: a red marking, a certain sound, a distinctive odor. Surely we, too, are in some ways "programmed" to respond to what we think of as beauty (a visual signal), to words (a sound signal), and to agreeable odors. We cannot judge to what extent our own responses may be equated with those of other animals, and to a large extent the reason for this is our imagination.

Fantasy

It is hard to tell where imagination ends and fantasy begins. Ordinarily we call fantasy an experience that takes place in the mind and cannot occur in reality. The brain has a tendency to fulfill unsatisfied bodily drives by this means, because an unsatisfied drive is experienced as a discomfort—pain, longing, tension, constriction—that interferes with the brain's smooth functioning. When any need becomes too intense, a self-corrective action must come into play; otherwise the brain would be preoccupied with it and unable to direct the other functions of the body.

Initially the fantasy assuages the need, but the underlying demand remains, and it becomes more urgent as time goes on. In the long run all the fantasy can do is to help postpone its gratification. Fantasy of this kind might be defined as a temporary alleviation of a commanding need. It goes without saying that there are other kinds of fantasy: flights of fancy, creative images, and so on. The word is used loosely and has several connotations to us, but here we are concerned with the dreams and ideas that substitute for reality.

A young woman who believes herself to be unattractive, whether this is objectively the case or not, will think that all the other girls she knows are prettier or brighter or in some way more desirable than she. This feeling will make her awkward in the company of young men, and the awkwardness itself is likely to contribute to a lack of success with them. This self-perpetuating series either serves to root more deeply her feeling of being unattractive or, alternatively, leads to a sour-grapes feeling toward men. "Who needs them?" she will say.

Sometimes a girl with these feelings finds solace in eating, eventually developing a layer of fat that figuratively and literally separates her from social contact. Her guiding motivation is her fear of rebuff. In becoming obese she removes the possibility of experiencing this kind of pain, because she takes herself right out of the social contest. ("How can I go to the dance? I can't find a dress that fits me.") Once she is safe from the temptation to enter into the social life of her group she can indulge in daydreams. She tells herself that all she has to do is lose all that weight and then she would have no trouble at all attracting all the "groovy guys." This, it goes without saying, is her fantasy, because she does not dare to put her assumption to the test. What if really she were slim and still failed to attract any boys? It would be so devastating that she cannot allow herself even to think about it. She spends a lifetime dieting, working off a few pounds and eating them back on again, thus holding onto her dream of how attractive she will be the day she is slim again. To put this into biological terms, she has been able to transmute her fear of being a loser into a pseudovictory. She does not win the rewards of real victory in social competition—status, a mate, children—but a pseudoreward: she may always live in the belief that these can be hers at any time she chooses to compete for them.

The numbers of ways in which fantasy can enter into the realm of sex are almost without end. Without fantasy, human sexual deviance could hardly exist. The word *deviance,* of course, is barely definable, since what is considered deviant is influenced by culture, and we are not going to attempt to define it here. Our object here is to draw attention to the part played by fantasy in unusual sexual practices. This is probably best exemplified by fetishism.

In fetishism a person, almost invariably a man, becomes sexually excited by a personal belonging, usually a piece of clothing belonging to the opposite sex. His fantasy supplies the missing woman. For reasons that have to do with the development of his psychological makeup during his period of growth, he cannot bring himself to face a real woman in a sexual relationship. Wide though the difference in their ultimate behavior is, the motivation of such a man is not dissimilar from that of the obese girl. Feeling insecure about his status as a male, he does not dare to put himself into a situation where he might suffer the unbearable pain of rebuff, and so he avoids this, as the fat girl does, by withdrawing from any contest. On the other hand his basic drives make demands that eventually, in some way or other, have to be met.

That people find varying solutions to this problem is a consequence of chance occurrences in their childhoods that cause them to associate some particular object with the sexual act. We can illustrate this with the case of a young man who masturbated to the fantasied image of a pair of man's shoes. It was discovered that as a child the door between his room and his parents' being ajar, he had become aware of the sexual activity of his parents while all he could see were his father's shoes under their bed. Those shoes became indelibly associated in his mind with sex, and so it happened that when, as he grew up, he felt inadequate to seek a woman as an object of love, it was the memory of those shoes that stimulated him.

For other individuals, other objects have a similar effect. Lacy lingerie and stockings have more obvious sexual connotations, but the feeling of inadequacy in the performer and the substitution of the "fetish" for the woman herself remains the same.

Dr. H. T. Buckner, a sociologist investigating the careers of trans-vestites, became aware that they had all experienced a sense of failure in activities that seemed to them masculine, particularly sports, sex-uality, or work. In his report he mentioned that transvestism seemed to be a way of saying to the world, "You are asking too much of me." Fantasy then leads them to think of themselves as in some way female, so as to enable them to satisfy their sexual needs in a way that is not threatening to them.

This kind of deviation points up how deeply ingrained is the importance of status to a human being. When confronted with a necessity for asserting their identity as a male and thus risking the possibility of failure, the transvestites prefer to sacrifice their mascu-line role.

The same problem—the feeling of inadequacy—is also at the root of behavior in the more extreme forms of deviance, such as pedophil-ism or even necrophilism.

Thus fantasy comes to the rescue of the person lacking self-confi-dence and permits him to avoid the contest whose outcome he dreads. Should a man with this kind of personality makeup be persuaded to put himself to the test and should he then find himself indeed to be a loser, the consequence would be a depression of extreme severity and perhaps suicide.

Fantasy can also play a negative role. When a man's upbringing creates in him a feeling that women are all-powerful creatures that he cannot possibly conquer, this clearly will affect his sexuality when he is older with or without the intervention of his fantasy. But in more extreme cases in which, say, a mother is cruel and physically abu-sive—in which she berates and hits, or throws objects at the father, in which she abuses and beats her son—this boy may grow up with a fantasy of all women as witches or as fire-breathing dragons. If he does, when he is grown up he obviously will not be able to love any woman.

The sex drive is not diminished in such a man, but for him the object of his drive is a person he fears so strongly that he feels she may be a threat to his life. When seized by a powerful sexual urge he almost automatically puts a weapon in his pocket and goes on the prowl. In the struggle that ensues, his delusion tells him that he is fighting a being who will destroy him if he does not kill her. When the feared creature lies helpless, his sense of triumph over her, added to the sexual impulse that prompted the aggression in the first place, stokes his sense of mastery, and he is able to rape her when she is dying or dead, although he would have been totally unable to perform sexually with her alive. Such a man's fantasy of conquering a powerful opponent, delusionary as it is, opens the only way to sexual function possible for him.

Havelock Ellis noted that sexual release may come through acts of violence. He averred that the innocent "love bite" and the violence of "Jack the Ripper" were varying degrees of the same impulse. The Kinsey Institute studies found that thirty percent of rapists enjoyed beating their victims more than the actual intercourse. In many cases the rapist is impotent. Mutilation, stabbing, or strangulation of women, they stated, is related to a basically frightened man with concerns about his masculinity and fears of women.

Aggressive and violent as the acts of such persons are, they stand completely outside the competitiveness and aggression that are associated with sexuality in the natural order. No competition is involved with others of the same sex to demonstrate prowess. The deviant is not competing with anything except a figment of his own fantasy. And what removes his act even further from natural status struggles is the fact that he abides by no socially accepted rules.

In other acts of individual desperado a similar basic inadequacy has been recognized. *Time* magazine reported that "Charles Tuller, who led the band that took over the Eastern jet, could not sustain his marriage, hated his ex-wife, and was said to be awkward and uncomfortable around women." The same report mentioned that "the man who was subdued before he could hijack a National Airlines jet in New York was discovered to be wearing women's underclothes."

Dr. David Hubbard, a psychiatrist who has made a special study of skyjackers, has remarked that in his experience they are "not strong, masculine supermen but weak, longtime losers, men who have failed at life and love. They tend to be passive, effeminate, latently homosexual, and afraid of their eldest sisters and mothers."

When interviewed after capture many skyjackers have confessed, "I never dated. I didn't know how to ask." "When a skyjacker gets married," Dr. Hubbard said, "it is usually to a woman who seduced him first and proposed later. Almost without exception the men were

reviled by their wives, strove to placate them, and were often cuckolded. One betrayed skyjacker's wife told her husband that he had
never pleased her, had a tiny penis, and not the least idea what to do
with it."

The obvious explanation for the subsequent violence is that the
husband, shattered by that kind of accusation, tries to repair his ego by
the daring act of air piracy. But it can also be seen as a striving for rank
on a par with the adolescent who yells to the gang of boys that has
been tormenting him, "Just who do you think you are? I'm as good as
any of you—in fact, I'm better. See, I can jump from the highest
window." And if he breaks his leg in doing so he feels it was worthwhile to have had his moment of glory—rank—when he commanded
everyone's attention.

Another negative expression of sexual fantasy is jealousy, especially jealousy aroused by insufficient grounds or where there are no
grounds for it at all. Jealousy is an emotion that looms large in human
nature, and for that reason it has served as a theme for countless
writers who have been fascinated by its sometimes extreme consequences.

Jealousy intrigues us too, for it has a facet that fits right into the
theme of this chapter in that the mind and its fantasies play a para-
mount role in its creation. It is incredible with what minutiae the
mind of the jealous person can build up an image of his beloved lying
in the arms of another and then invoke all his resources of observation
and reason to marshal supporting clues, even when the mental image
of the presumed infidelity happens to be entirely without foundation.
Deductive abilities are put into the service of finding corroborating
evidence, piecing together "evidence" with the flimsiest of "clues."

There is a young man who in his college years was a prominent
athlete and very popular. He was a rather indifferent student, but this
didn't trouble him. One of the girls he knew, who was quiet and
unassuming but an exceptionally good student, got into the habit of
helping him with his courses, suggesting ideas, and typing his papers.
This led to the natural outcome: they got used to each other and
eventually married.

After marriage, in building up a career, his athletic prowess no
longer supported his self-esteem, and he began to question his other
abilities. As he did so, he felt his first twinges of doubt about his
relationship with his wife, who by then was working as an assistant to

one of her old professors. When she talked to him about her work with enthusiasm, he was inclined to scoff at the people she mentioned and their work ("Who's interested in medieval English?" or "What possible use does all that have for anyone today?"). Later on, when she began to invite some of her colleagues home, he felt left out and became morose, particularly when there was laughter over something he didn't understand. He began to resent her intellectual intimacy with these people, and it was then that his fantasy started to build up the mental picture of a rival or rivals that by slow degrees incited him to scenes of intense jealousy.

He questioned her closely whenever she was a few minutes late but did not believe her replies; he left his work early to hide in the vicinity of her office in the hope (or fear) of discovering which of her colleagues was more than just that; he made frequent telephone calls to check up on her. As his conviction of her infidelity came to fill his mind, he lost all interest in sexual activity. (Below the level of his conscious thought he was actually rejecting her in advance, because he believed she was about to reject him or at least to compare him unfavorably with her "lovers.")

He was unable to concentrate on anything else. When people talked to him he hardly heard what they said. His work suffered. Closer to his conscious mind, but never expressed aloud, his thoughts ran on and on like a broken record: Who the hell does she think she is?—she's not even pretty—she can't even cook a decent meal—if I didn't tell her what to get we'd be eating the same old stew every day—I've had it up to here—I don't need a bookworm, I need a woman—Why did I let her do my work at school?—I should have done it myself and I'd know more now—I was a damn fool for not putting my foot down—maybe I'm just plain stupid—I was stupid enough to marry her, wasn't I? . . .

What he did express out loud were venomous accusations.

His wife was totally unaware of what was going on in his mind or what caused his jealousy. At first she thought it was because he loved her very much, and she was rather flattered. Later, as his jealousy came to be accompanied by expressions of hatred, she was at a loss. Nothing seemed to appease him, even her offer to leave her job. It was only when they sought help that the actual issues crystallized out of the misleading fantasy and the resulting welter of false accusations.

The young husband had been a high-ranking male in his school years, but his area of excellence was irrelevant in the society in which he found himself after he married. The conventional competition of that group was in the sphere of mental agility. He was like a rooster displaying a handsome red comb before a company of peacocks who could only be impressed by brilliant back feathers. Under ordinary circumstances he might have found his level in such a group, but when this problem was combined with the difficulties he was experiencing in beginning his career he felt like a failure. The fantasies his brain produced at this stage may have helped to salve his pride ("It is not I who am unmanly—it is she who is unworthy"), but they wreaked havoc in his marriage.

The jealous delusions conjured up by the brain can go to grotesque extremes. One elderly man, whose feelings of inadequacy also led him to drink too much, was driven by a mechanism similar to this young husband's. Imagining that his wife indulged in all kinds of escapades, he made her life miserable with his jealous accusations, in spite of the fact that she was partly crippled and confined to a wheelchair!

In these examples we have illustrations of how man's most prized possession, his brain, in defending its own function sometimes interferes with the effective working of his natural drives.

Judgment

In the matter of sex, judgment could refer to the basic question: whether sex is, so to speak, "good" or "bad." It is not this kind of judgment, however, that we are going to explore here, for this realm belongs to the social historian, to the theologian, or to the philosopher.

Our subject at this point is what might be called Sex as a Competitive Sport. As in any sport, its performance has become subject to self-judgment and the judgment of others.

As we have said, in the rest of the animal world and in the cultures of tribal man, the privilege of reproducing one's kind was a prize to be competed for. The young male had to prove himself, to gain status among males, before he was deemed fit to take a wife. And a young female had to possess status among females. The union of the two young people who had thus proved themselves fit then had a good chance of being as stable as local ingenuity could devise.

In our Western societies today, by contrast, the preliminary competition has been reduced to a minimum, and the prize, sex itself, has become the arena. The young male, eyeing an eligible female, asks himself not whether she will be able to cook his dinner, darn his socks, or raise his children, but, "Is she sexy?" And the young female, debating whether to encourage the advances of the male, does not consider whether he will be able to provide her the wherewithal to do these things, but, "Does he send me?"

Such an elimination from the contest of the preliminary heats carries its own penalties. The most obvious are those that result after the pleasures of the marriage bed have been dulled by routine and the male is revealed as an irresponsible provider or the female as incapable of maintaining the comfort of the home or raising the children.

But even if by luck the male should prove to be a munificent provider and the female a paragon of domestic virtue, the less obvious penalty remains. By removing the contest from the qualifying rounds and concentrating upon the race itself, modern men and women are left with the perennial gnawing doubt, "Am I good in bed?" It is hardly possible for such worries to be laid to rest, for even if they are put into tentative words ("Do I make you happy, honey?"), what is the partner to say? The sturdiest affirmation may be only half-believed by the self-doubter. On the other hand a bald statement that "John [or Joan] is much better than you are" would reduce what little confidence the partner had to the level of zero.

It is here that the purely cerebral element, judgment, enters the picture, for there are no absolutes in a contest of this sort. What pleases one woman may not please another, and what one man judges good another may find distasteful. A human male cannot, so to say, display his plumage with confidence, for, metaphorically, how is he to know if it is the right color? How is a human female, worried about her mate's judgment of her sexual performance, to rate herself?

The need for criteria in this area is apparently so dire that it has occasioned the emergence of an (almost) entirely new category of popular literature, the sex manual. This handy reference book sets up objectives in terms of what a person ought to expect; suggests both conventional techniques and surprise tactics that might prove successful ways of achieving orgasms; and provides advice to the novice as well as more advanced suggestions for the experienced, quite similar to the advice offered the bridge player or golfer in the various manuals that are available to aid in improving performance in those games.

The intense need of the modern male or female for a conviction of personal competence in the Olympics of sex is indicated by the extent and variety of the instruction offered. The sex manual is not alone in the field. Some enterprising firms offer illustrated lectures in the form of home movies. Many schools and universities offer open courses or private counseling. Private practitioners in the counseling field know no off season for their services. Research groups investigate the manifestations of this basic drive, and medical groups propagate specialized techniques for the sexually handicapped. Even the adviser himself or herself is not immune. Magazines, some of high quality, are published for the enlightenment of doctors in all that pertains to human sexuality, and the doctors are caught up in the all-pervasive feeling of the necessity for omniscience in the area.

The reader who has followed us thus far is aware of how far off the mark is all this instruction in sexual technique, whether by manual, motion picture, or medical lecture. Being told what to do and how to do it does not help the body to produce the responses that eventually find expression in the sexual act. It is almost like attempting to teach an art student by showing him how to produce a variety of brush strokes when he has no idea of the picture he wants to paint. Where effort is confined to making boys and girls confident of themselves in their masculinity and femininity, sexual responses follow automatically. These boys and girls will have gleaned enough from what they have observed from the adults around them during their growing years to guide them along the lines that are acceptable to their societies. Differences in technique have never been a factor in the end result of producing a new generation, and whether or not they add to the sum total of human pleasure is a dubious question.

Let us hasten to state that neither of us believes that sex should be purely functional and without pleasure to the participants. On the contrary, we are entirely in favor of any form of activity that adds pleasure to our lives, but the stresses, self-doubts, anxieties, and outright malfunctions that are consequences of the present insistence upon sexual intercourse as an area for conventional competition seem to us totally unjustified by the very slight difference technique makes to the ultimate sense of pleasure.

One plus that we may grant the sex manuals is that they do indeed provide many a fillip to the imagination, and, as we have said, the imagination plays a large role in human love. But is this fillip worth the consequence the whole game engenders?

Who, after all, are the readers of the sex manuals or the audiences of the counselors? They are those who feel insecure in their sexuality. Indeed, they usually are insecure in their total personality, but they focus on their sexuality as the core of their problem. Faced with the seemingly overwhelming complications of the skill in which they have judged themselves to be deficient, many give up in despair. They believe that every normal person is capable of performing the recommended athletics, and this confirms their own judgment of themselves as inadequate. Thus for the majority of their readers (for the self-confident don't trouble to look at them), the sex manuals defeat their avowed purpose in that they leave the unconfident judging themselves even more harshly than they did before they opened the book and thereby even further incapacitated.

14

Variations on a Theme

An ability to respond to stimuli is as basic to all life as the ability for self-reproduction. There is no living thing that does not have these two capacities.

In the course of evolution the nervous system developed as an organ to channel an animal's responses to stimuli into actions that would be conducive to its survival. The earliest rudimentary nervous apparatus was slowly refined, first into the ganglionic nervous systems that still serve invertebrates and then into the brains of higher animals. In each species of higher animal certain parts of the brain then developed to an especially high degree, initially because it was the most useful in aiding the survival of that species. In some it was the part of the brain governing the sense of smell, the so-called olfactory brain; in others it was the part governing sight or hearing or those special senses like echo location in bats or the capacity for direction finding (navigation) in birds. In each case the high degree of development of the certain part of the brain occurred because it was useful and was retained by selection, but it then became a governing element in the creature's life. Bats, which have survived as species because of their ability to perceive the world by echo location, eventually lead lives based on that special sense: all their awareness is determined by it.

In our species the part of the brain that is especially highly developed is the neocortex, the reasoning, judging part that we sometimes refer to loosely as "the mind" to distinguish it from the parts that govern our more automatic functions. Because of this, the influence of the thinking mind over each and every phase of our functioning is so all-pervasive that one can only give the barest indication of the directions into which it leads us. We have just been discussing some of these, particularly those directions that influence sexual function or dysfunction, since that is our present theme. At the same time we must always keep in mind the fact that although almost everything we do has some element of our "special brain" in it, we all also retain the old brain that we have inherited from the beginning of time, that has all the experiences of our evolutionary history programmed into it, and that governs all our deepest feelings.

Having just indicated some few of the directions into which our neocortex may lead us, we now want to examine a few of the variations on the theme of sex and status that are to be found in our species because of our possession of a mind, or perhaps it would be more accurate to say, because our thinking minds cannot always accept the solution that our older brains urge upon us.

Preventive Impotence

Social impotence and sexual impotence are first cousins; indeed, sometimes these states are so closely interwoven that it might be more accurate to call them twins.

Competition is one of life's basic ingredients: it is the inevitable result of the overproduction of offspring of which every single species is capable, and it provides the mechanism whereby species may refine their forms and behavior in the direction of even greater adaptation. Nonetheless, it is possible to some degree and in certain circumstances to block, and perhaps to breed out, competition. We do it with our domestic pets, and some of us do it with our children.

The means we use to do this is overprotection, and it takes a high degree of overprotection to achieve this. For domestic cattle, sheep, pigs, or poultry we provide an abundance of food, which might be expected to lead to an absence of competition for it, and security from predators, which one might think would remove the need for competition to establish leaders and followers. But this is not the case. Strong dominance structures have been observed among all these domestic animals. Only when we remove individual animals from the company of their own kind, take them into our houses as family pets, and treat them as individuals do we manage to eliminate their natural competitiveness (although, obviously, this is not our objective).

The owner of a pet or, for that matter, any person who takes on a parental attitude has to adopt unwaveringly a very specific course to thwart the animal's (or the child's) inherent competitive tendency. Some adults, because of their own immature needs, have a desire to maintain an intensely close, loving relationship with another creature. By performing services for that creature, whether pet or child, that it is actually able to perform for itself, they delay the development of its social maturity and tie it to themselves with silken bonds of mutual love and dependence. Others may take recourse to threats: "If you don't do what I want you to do, I won't love you anymore." This threat, spoken or implied, may lead to such a feeling of insecurity in the child (or pet) that it gives the "parent" all the love and duty the parent desires in order not to risk abandonment. Either path—that of oversolicitousness, or that of threat or inducing feelings of guilt—effectively destroys in the child the belief that it can compete and in the animal the ability to compete.

There are other ways of arriving at this end. A parent's persistent inconsistency in attitudes and, more subtle but even more damaging, constantly saying one thing and doing or meaning another can totally undermine the capacity for independent action in the developing creature. Never knowing what will be approved or disapproved, the child or pet does not dare to experiment, put curiosity to the test, or try out alternatives—the chief routes to a secure sense of independence—but gradually becomes an adult without self-confidence or a cowed and fawning animal.

There are many adults among us who fear responsibility and social commitment, such as assuming initiative or becoming involved in relationships that might lead to marriage. Such people eschew all kinds of contest; their minds and bodies have not learned to coordinate the necessary responses for competition. They are so convinced they *cannot* compete that they experience an intense fear of being shamed or ridiculed whenever they face a situation that they feel to be competitive. They will use any means to avoid the contest.

Because such a person feels he cannot win, he prefers not to compete at all. He cultivates the "loser" complex and takes on the role of loser without even fighting. Thus the attributes of a loser become incorporated into his personality and serve as an adaptive mechanism that saves him the pain of actually experiencing loss of face. Avoidance becomes the keynote of his life. Usually he will develop a philosophy of existence that to him justifies nonparticipation. He may follow those Oriental teachings that advocate withdrawal from worldly ambition, religious principles about the vanity of the world and the supreme value of the hereafter, or secular ideals of universal brotherhood, or he may disqualify himself by obesity, hypochondriasis, or sexual impotence. Which path he takes is of secondary importance: it is determined by the chance circumstances of his individual life. What *is* significant is the factor of *avoidance* that underlies all the paths. There are countless variations of this theme, but in whichever key it is played the melody is the same. One variation of avoidance of sexual responsibility, and one that is frequently encountered, is premature ejaculation.

In the experience of André, a postgraduate student who suffered from this disability, we can see the complexity of the factors that led to it. His father, mother, friends, school—any one of which alone would have been sufficient—all played a part in his general feeling of inadequacy. In his case a Freudian psychologist could easily find the source of his difficulty in a "castration anxiety."

André's mother was oversolicitous and inordinately proud of her only offspring. She had him tutored in attention-getting skills. By the time he was six he could play the piano, tap dance, and recite. He was her joy and the envy of all her friends. She herself was a socially ambitious person, but she lacked the self-discipline to see a project through to completion. She had followed many successive pursuits, but in her impatience to achieve excellence speedily she lost interest before she could prove herself in any of them. And where she herself could not succeed she expected, practically demanded, that either her husband or André fill the gap for her, so that she could shine through them.

Her husband was a stodgy and rather unimaginative businessman who took her prodding with conspicuous resignation, but occasionally, when it became too much for him, he exploded into rage. These scenes sent shudders through André's whole being: he feared his father might actually kill his mother.

His mother was very demonstrative in her affection for André, and this made him most uncomfortable. In his dependence on her, however, he desired above all not to offend her, and he strove to do whatever he could to please her. Therefore he made no attempt to extricate himself from her embraces. Here was a perfect example of what the Freudians view as the classic triangle. The father was not the object of the mother's love. She turned to the boy for fulfillment, and to him the father loomed as a threatening figure in the background. This could have been mitigated had André been able to identify with his father, but unfortunately he could not. He was sensitive and artistically inclined, and he could not see any merit in the pragmatic standards of a businessman. He often had an urge to protect his mother from his father's rages and from his insensitivity toward her. Although André never experienced any fear that his father might deprive him of his masculinity either symbolically or literally, a Freudian could explain André's sexual predicament as an unconscious castration anxiety.

An Adlerian psychologist would see André as a victim of an overwhelming feeling of inferiority that precluded any sense of power. He had never been permitted to, and could not, participate in rough-and-tumble games with other boys. Later, believing that he did not possess the necessary skills, he shunned sports. Perhaps to compensate, his fantasies abounded with glorious deeds. Any report in the news of daredevil or heroic deeds sparked his imagination like Walter Mitty's. In his chosen fields of music and theater, where he felt more secure, he fell into the same pattern as his mother's and abandoned attempts because he could not succeed fast enough. His dreams of glory prevented him from being satisfied with his actual achievements, which were not small, and therefore these activities did not afford him any compensation for those more vigorous ones that were beyond his power.

But when we look at André from a standpoint of evolutionary psychology it becomes clear that he was a subordinate creature his entire life. His mother babied him and made decisions for him. His father was distant and fear inspiring, so that he could never feel strong enough to challenge him. At first he had no opportunity to compete with his peers, and later he shunned them. Another person might have accepted this subordinate role and felt contented in it, but he could not. He felt defeated without even having engaged in any contest that could justify it. As a result, in his eyes, any woman had a rank superior to his own. She could command him in any way she pleased.

In his feelings, an embrace was tantamount to an order that he offer her what is required in such a situation, and his body responded automatically. With a strange feeling of detachment, almost as though he were not there, he dutifully ejaculated the way an obedient servant would carry out the order of his master, without the slightest hesitation. In fact he mentioned that in some of his fantasies he saw himself captured by Amazons and made their slave, but even then his fancy did not envision sexual relations; rather he saw himself being milked every morning, rather like a cow, so they could use the product of his masculinity for the creation of offspring.

André confided his predicament to his mother, who then told him that his father had the same problem. She made exhaustive inquiries and selected for him a very capable Freudian analyst. André related to this man well. He tried to please him as he tried to please any adult of superior standing. He read his way through numerous books on psychology and gained an exceptional understanding of his problems. He felt comfortable and secure with his doctor. His difficulties with his girls, however, remained unchanged.

After one and a half years André's analysis came to a sudden halt when his doctor became seriously ill. André himself would have been content to let matters rest, but his mother, who was already dissatisfied with his progress, took advantage of the opportunity and contacted an Adlerian psychologist. In the meantime she too had immersed herself in psychological literature and had taken courses on the subject.

André had an even greater rapport with his new doctor than with the old one, but the same pattern was repeated. No changes took place either in his attitude toward a career (he remained an eternal student) or with his sexual problem. Finally the doctor suggested that André would be better off if he were to leave his home and continue his studies somewhere else.

His mother cheerfully accepted this new challenge. She made numerous inquiries, selected a school, and typed out his applications. When he was accepted she traveled to that distant city and found an apartment for him near the school. She then bought a ticket for him and sent him off.

André roomed with two other students, and he quickly became the maid. Gladly he did the shopping, cleaning, and cooking and took their numerous telephone messages, mostly from girls. A few blind dates arranged for him by his roommates had the same embarrassing consequences: instantaneous ejaculation. One of the girls, a frequent visitor to the apartment, took a motherly interest in him, and before long he told her about his failing. As though in an unchanging script she, too, arranged an appointment for him with a psychiatrist.

The new doctor was an eclectic: he attempted to use whatever methods seemed appropriate to the patient's individual needs and was not bound to any particular school of thought. From the very first session André tried to be a good patient, but to his consternation this doctor would not accept his kind of docility. He encouraged André to challenge him on any issue, point, or wording if he did not agree with it. After the introductory interview his sexual difficulty was not discussed at all. All the conversation was directed toward the resources of character and skill that André possessed and how best to use them, even though he would hardly acknowledge that he had any at all and was made very anxious by the mere thought of any change in his style of life.

Since he was in any case doing all the cooking for himself and his roommates, his doctor suggested that he make a virtue out of it. He encouraged him to read more on cooking and try out elaborate recipes. Before long he became really proud of his culinary achievements. They turned out so well he called them "eye poppers," and his fame spread among his fellow students. They began to vie for his invitations. For the first time in his life he knew what it meant to hold rank. As far as he was concerned he was the number one chef. For him it was his first contest, and he had won it. When his guests oohed and ahed over his gastronomic feats he realized a sense of triumph he had never experienced before. He even had a feeling of condescension when he explained the finer points of a dish to a girl who was ignorant about such an important matter.

Little by little it dawned on him that he had never accepted challenges, had not given himself any chance to prove whether he could make the grade or not. He also began to realize that one has to be realistic about one's own achievements: that one cannot win in every field, but that one doesn't have to be a superman to gain recognition in some area. Ultimately he understood that it was not what he did but the way he felt about it that made the difference. He could easily have scoffed at being a good cook, and that would have destroyed the pleasure he derived from his skill.

André's original desire to be associated with the theater finally focused on becoming a stage manager. After a short apprenticeship he savored the feeling of being in command of a group of actors. It was then that he made his first serious attempt to date again. Forewarned not to fall into the trap of placing himself in a subordinate position, he began to date Jacqueline, a young aspiring actress who appeared to him an ideal companion. Aware now of the disastrous consequence that would ensue if he were to fall into his old role of the good fellow, always helpful and accommodating, he began to make demands on Jacqueline. Much to his surprise, she was cheerfully obliging. He confided in her his problem of always having felt obliged to assume the subordinate role, and she was understanding because she, too, had had similar problems. The two young people literally practiced how to assert themselves with each other. Their newly found confidence quickly spilled over into other areas of their lives, and André finally was able to feel equal with his contemporaries. It was quite a while after he had achieved satisfactory genital function that he rather casually mentioned this to his doctor.

André's premature, or in his case instantaneous, ejaculation was no more a sexual problem than was the obese girl's a metabolic one.

In diseases of childhood like measles the symptom we see is the rash on the skin, but the skin rash is not the disease. It is simply one of the outward expressions that let us know the disease is there. To cure it we do not treat the skin, but we attempt to neutralize the virus that brings the condition into being. In about the same way, most sexual dysfunctions are manifestations of underlying social problems, and to remedy them it is the underlying problem that must be tackled rather than its outward expression. When the primary cause is a disease, the same holds true. If diabetes brings impotence in its wake, we treat the diabetes.

Naturally there are some instances in which the outward symptom is so troubling that some relief must be provided, much as one would attempt to relieve excessive skin irritation with a dusting of powder, but the basic problem has to be dealt with before a lasting improvement can take place. Today it is rare to find sexual problems caused by total ignorance. Of course, if such an instance should present itself then there is no alternative but to offer instruction, but it is our experience that in all the cases we have encountered of so-called ignorance, this itself has proved to be a mask for socially induced fear.

In the examples we have given of underlying personal insecurity masked by obesity, fetishism, jealousy, impotence, or even emerging in criminality, the outward symptoms are not merely a consequence of fear of social competition. The symptoms themselves become factors that reinforce the feelings of inadequacy that the victims had in the first place. Like a wheel turning uselessly on a muddy road, the symptoms drive them deeper into the condition from which they suffer.

Such people usually accept their lot. They live restricted lives and seldom seek psychiatric help unless they are pushed to it by relatives or friends. The true nature of their problem often reveals itself only when other difficulties arise, as they often do in such personalities. In seeking help for that other thing, this defensive mechanism is then uncovered.

In one case a woman sought advice because she wanted to avoid the breakup of her marriage. She was completely unaware of any sexual problem and believed that her difficulties arose from her husband's unreasonable attitude.

Lisa was a chemical engineer who had grown up and studied in Munich. She was a dedicated worker. Although to outward appearances she seemed to lack imagination, she often had original ideas but kept them to herself, only to see others putting similar thoughts into practice later on and reaping the acclaim they deserved. She was quiet and unobtrusive, with a permanently fixed slight smile that revealed neither pleasure nor sadness, but rather a desire not to offend. In her schooldays in Munich her marks had never reflected the amount of work she put in nor the knowledge she possessed. Examinations, whether oral or written, made her so anxious that she was not able to reveal the quality of her work or thought. But in spite of this she put herself wholeheartedly into her work, if for no other reason than that her life at home was rather dreary and her work was her only interest. She had had a brief romance during her final year at school, but it had left her with a never completely healed wound. She had lived with her parents and two younger brothers in a very small house, where the only part she could call her own was a tiny attic room. Her father, a typical petty tyrant, was never satisfied with anything. He constantly found fault with Lisa's mother and with his own mother, who was a frequent visitor to the house. He had very little regard for women in general, and he extended this lack of regard to Lisa, often saying that he did not consider her intelligent enough to justify letting her go on to the university. It says a lot for her innate capacities that this kind of treatment did not prevent her from being able to cope with her chosen work, but it did leave its imprint on her personality: it left her with a permanent feeling of little worth. It was no wonder that when she received an offer for a job abroad soon after obtaining her degree, she accepted it promptly.

Lisa was rather lonely in her new environment. She was not able to participate in the banter and camaraderie of the office, and she was frequently teased in a good-natured way. This made it doubly difficult for her to bring herself to make the acquaintance of Bruce, who worked in an adjoining office.

But Bruce must have felt her interest in him, and he began to pay attention to her. He was a divorced man with two children, and he had left his wife because she was always "depressed." He said he wanted to have a little joy in life and not always have to come home after a hard day's work to a "sad sack" who had nothing happy to tell him about each day's events. He found Lisa's foreign background and soft-spoken ways charming, and eventually their romance culminated in marriage.

From the beginning Lisa noticed that Bruce's mood changed after every sexual union. He became brusque and carping, although at other times he was loving and attentive. She told herself, "Probably that's the way all men are," but just the same she had a feeling that something was wrong. Being inexperienced and too self-conscious to inquire about the mood changes just at those times, she redoubled her efforts to please Bruce in any way she could think of. But none of this helped, and he began to find excuses for coming home later and later. Most painful to her, he completely ignored her at the office. It was her feeling that she was to blame for whatever was wrong with her marriage, and now that the evidence of their unhappiness was being brought into the office she thought her colleagues would be confirmed in their opinions (which she presumed they held all along) that she was not suited to be a wife.

Eventually Bruce told her that he had found another woman and that he wanted to end their marriage. Of all the pains she had ever experienced this was the worst. She was near collapse, but somehow the intensity of her despair gave her a modicum of strength. With an unaccustomed insistence she persuaded Bruce to go with her to their minister. The clergyman, correctly surmising that more was involved than fell within his province, advised them to seek professional help together.

Bruce was willing to do this. In spite of what had passed between them he still felt affection and respect for Lisa, and he welcomed the opportunity to lay his feelings bare in her presence. He had come to believe that he could not satisfy Lisa sexually. It seemed to him that she barely tolerated his advances and that it was only because she was a kind person that she neither rejected them nor complained. He said that no matter how hard he tried he could not arouse her, that he blamed himself, and that he felt like a total failure as a man. He went on that it was only to reassure himself that he had started the affair and that he did not even find the woman attractive. She was a widow; she was much more responsive to him sexually than he had believed was still possible for him, but this didn't mean too much to him because he placed her in a much lower category than Lisa.

Lisa listened to this outpouring with obvious incredulity, as though she totally disbelieved her own ears. Whenever she had a chance she interrupted, "But I do love you." It became clear that she was totally unaware of the fact that she was frigid and that it was useless to try to explain this to her, because her only response would have been to reiterate that it couldn't be possible because she loved him. She passionately insisted that she would sacrifice anything to make him happy.

Lisa was encouraged to think about the role she assumed in any human group. In spite of her educational achievement and professional standing, she invariably placed herself in a subordinate position to anyone who crossed her path. Even her occasional maid largely disregarded her requests, and Lisa, although dissatisfied with her work, did not dare to dismiss her. In her own career she had never pressed for raises in salary or for advancement, and as a result she had often had to stand by and see less deserving coworkers obtain recognition that rightfully should have come to her first. She had a ready explanation for her reticence: "It isn't right to push oneself forward, and anyway, people don't like you if you try to impose on them." But when she gave this a little more thought she added, "To be honest, I really would love to be the kind of person who could have the courage to walk into the director's office and talk to him as though he were a member of the family." To take such a step would have caused her untold embarrassment. She thought she would surely be rebuffed: how dare she be so familiar with someone superior to herself? As she was relating this thought, it dawned on her that this was the kind of language her father had used. Implied in all his mutterings ran the theme that women were inferior, and this ingrained assumption influenced her whenever she was in the company of other people. When she was confronted with a plain question, "How can you, as a scientist, accept such a contention?" she smiled, realizing for the first time the monstrous burden she had carried.

With this understanding, she was able to give vent to feelings and thoughts she had always had, but never discussed because she hadn't considered them subjects for discussion. They might have sounded like complaints, and she didn't think it was seemly for a woman to mention such things. She had considered it a woman's lot to be of service to a man and in sex to offer her body for his gratification. As she was saying this she stopped, wondering how she, an educated and intelligent woman, could conceivably have accepted such a view. Searching within herself she admitted that she found such a state of affairs revolting and, probably, that was the reason she had shunned male companionship most of her life. She finally burst out that, yes, she had always been angry, but had not dared to show how she felt in fear of suffering consequences. Suddenly she was able to grasp the nature of her problem: while her mind was proclaiming love for her husband, her body was expressing her anger at him for the inferior role that men had assigned to women.

"Suppose you permit yourself the luxury of disagreeing with Bruce or even telling him off if you think he is unfair to you, do you actually believe he would either destroy you or walk away from you?" she was asked. "Suppose you tell your maid that if she wants to keep her job you expect her to show you the respect that is due you, would you feel that you may destroy her and that she could not recuperate from the blow?" Without answering the questions, she let their meaning sink in.

Slowly it seeped into Lisa's mind that all her life she had been playing out her father's script, with the effect of making her defend herself against men. She saw what had never crossed her mind before: that she was frigid and that her frigidity was in part protest and part protection against male dominance.

In the end her need for love asserted itself, but love could not thaw or even make her aware of her frigidity. Most importantly, she saw that the frigidity was not her basic problem, but that it was an outcome of the underdog role in which she had been cast and which she had *accepted*. As the long-suppressed anger surfaced she began to assert herself. One day, when Bruce took her maid's side in an inconsequential dispute, she became quite incensed. Bruce was nonplused and apologized. Lisa quickly eased the situation by laughing it off, but inwardly she experienced a wave of reassurance. She was a person to be reckoned with. That night the barrier that had held back her sexual impulses gave way.

Temporary Impotence

The body has many backup mechanisms. This has come about because as new organs and accretions developed in the course of evolution, on the whole they did not replace old ones but became added to them or engulfed them. The old organs retain their functions often unchanged, sometimes slightly modified by the newer parts.

Since we have developed in this way we are provided with a ready-made series of backup mechanisms when the later, more highly evolved structures and functions are damaged, meet difficulty, or for any other reason break down.

When anything impedes the decisions of our reasoning brain from being carried out, an older part of our brain, which governs our emotions, takes over. When this older part also, for any reason, is impeded, the very oldest part, which governs our automatic functions, then imposes its responses.

This series can be stated simply in the following terms:

Mechanism I. When we are in full possession of all our faculties, in a situation where it is possible to use them, we make a response promoted by logic.

Mechanism II. When it is not possible to use the dictates of logic (either because of physical damage to the brain or because the situation we are in precludes it), emotions take over and guide our behavior.

Mechanism III. When both these areas of the brain are put out of action, the autonomic core takes over; we then have a psychosomatic (vegetative) response.

The newer parts of our brains are clearly the more efficient. They have been selected by the pressures of countless ages precisely because they are so. This means that as we are obliged to fall back upon older mechanisms, our responses cannot help but be less efficient.

To have a very simple illustration of this, look at what happens if a traffic policeman errs, stops a motorist who has committed no offense, and proceeds to lecture him as though he had committed one. The first, and logical, response would be to explain reasonably to the policeman that he must have made a mistake, that the driver had committed no offense, and so on. But, as any motorist knows, there is not much future in an argument with a traffic policeman, and so the first logical response is suppressed.

Now the emotions assert themselves. The driver feels some anger. If he were able to defuse his anger with, perhaps, an expletive profanity, it would subside and leave him none the worse. But suppose his young daughter is sitting beside him as a passenger in his car. Then this harmless displacement is also denied him. His responses now have no means of external expression, and he will feel a general tension. As his brain suppresses his arm's readiness to punch, his leg's preparedness to kick, and the jaw's reflexive bite or snap, he will become uncomfortably aware of a stiffened back, clenched teeth, and a tightness in all the muscles that would promote these reactions. Moreover, his body will go on responding as though the punch, the kick, or the bite had actually been delivered. He will experience a heightening of his blood pressure. His heartbeat will be faster. Modern research has shown that in such circumstances all the body's systems that promote offense or defense are activated, while all those that are not essential to fight or flight (such as hunger, thirst, or sex) are inhibited.

The three mechanisms that we see in action in this example have an evolutionary history. It is now generally held that modern man's brain is essentially triune in nature. Although its parts are interconnected, they developed in different evolutionary stages and retain more or less separate functions. It has been possible to find out which activities are governed by the different parts of the brain by inflicting lesions on various parts and observing which areas of behavior are affected. Many such experiments have been made and corroborate these general statements.

All mammals still retain in the brain stem and its adjoining structures what was in effect the total brain apparatus of our reptilian forebears. Associated with this brain is imitative behavior, including courtship rituals, choices of places to eat, drink, and bask, migration, and similar stereotyped activities. In higher animals it may be important in choosing a home site and selecting leaders. It is important in man for ritualistic, repetitive behavior, compulsions, and a propensity to establish precedence.

Above the reptilian brain is the second part, which has been called the old mammalian brain or, more technically, the limbic system. This area is concerned with the emotions that establish mood and guide behavior. Of its three subdivisions two, concerned with feeding and sexual activity, are intimately associated with the olfactory apparatus, while the third, which is concerned with sociosexual behavior, is more closely connected with the visual system. The limbic system gets signals from the internal and external environment, and it contributes a great deal to feelings of personal identity.

The neocortex, or new mammalian brain, appeared late. It is closely associated with the outside world and concerned with abstracting the messages of the senses, with reason and judgment, and with the creation of ideas. It is very visual.

As we can see, aspects of our sexual behavior are monitored by all three parts of our brain, but the newest, what we call the "thinking" part, has come to dominate both the others. Thus, for our sexual apparatus to function smoothly our thoughts, values, beliefs, judgments, and ideas must be in harmony with our environment. When our ideals conflict with the situation in which we find ourselves, a condition of stress is set up. This drives us back on those older responses that are not within our conscious control and that may play havoc with our bodies in the form of psychosomatic ailments.

It has been amply demonstrated that stress dramatically reduces testosterone secretion in males. This does not prove that low testosterone levels cause the impotence, or temporary impotence, that is so often a concomitant of stress, but it does give an indication of internal turmoil. It also suggests that whatever causes the reduced testosterone production also causes the impotence, either directly or indirectly.

It has been noted, too, that stress has an overall depressing effect on most glandular secretions, and this fits into the processes of social order that we described earlier. Through the bodily manifestations of stress an animal defeated in conventional competition is inhibited from repeated contests, accepts the dominance of another animal, and is inclined to lose its sex drive. This leaves the winner free to go about breeding, protecting, and leading and ensures the harmony of the animal group until the next breeding season.

So far as the bodily responses are concerned, man experiences the same effects as other mammals. The complication that arises for man is that his more highly developed new brain (neocortex) does not invariably accept the responses promoted by the older part. Therefore he cannot accept feelings of lowered rank and impotence automatically, but experiences shame in fear of social opprobrium, depression, or alarm sometimes amounting to panic.

Sudden attacks of impotence plague men who are undergoing the stresses and strains of daily life, and they occur more frequently than is generally supposed—so frequently, in fact, that we have to consider them part of our cultural pattern.

One of the first things a man (and in many ways this applies to a woman too) notices when he is under stress is a falling off of sexual desire. He is less affectionate; he doesn't want to be bothered if his wife tries to cheer him up; he is irritable. Neither he nor anyone else would define this mood as impotence, but it is a precursor and actually a part of the whole picture. His own behavior begins to alarm him. He thinks something is physically wrong and goes to doctors for a physical checkup. Their reassurances that nothing is wrong with him do not relieve him. On the contrary, not being able to put a finger on the cause of his unease frightens him even more. Not infrequently he blames his misfortune on a woman. His wife is extravagant, and he has to work too hard to support his family. She is too busy with other things and doesn't pay attention to him. If she does pay attention to him he rejects her because she didn't pay attention yesterday and so on. Most wives who have had this experience could fill in this script. But however much he blames her for his mood, doubts about himself begin to seep into his mind and to build up. How was another man at his office able to pin down an account that he couldn't? Perhaps he is in the wrong profession; he is tired of the rat race. Should any of these vague fears be corroborated by external events, whether actual or in his imagination, then reason leaves him, and panic sets in. And with panic comes true impotence.

This is such a frequent event as to be almost trite. There is such a sameness about such stories that none of them really stands out. Yet to the person struck by this course of events, it is a most intense drama.

For example, Walter is a young, ambitious, and hard-driving person with a responsible position in an electronics firm. Recently he was in a quandary because he did not know whether or not to accept a new assignment to take charge of a small foreign subsidiary. A few years ago he would gladly have sold his soul to achieve this sort of goal, but now, with young children in school, a down payment made on a nice home, many friends and social ties in the neighborhood, it was the most difficult decision of his life. After many sleepless nights, he far from wholeheartedly arrived at a decision not to accept the offer. His superiors were very understanding, and it seemed to him, at least at first, that everything in his life was going on as usual. But a little later when a colleague of about his own rank was given a promotion, he began to become uneasy. He had the feeling that he should have been the first in line for the next available promotion, but then, when it came, it had gone to someone else. He made cautious inquiries and learned that the new opening was not one that could utilize his particular skills. This answer seemed reasonable, but it didn't quell his suspicions that something was amiss. The final blow came when one of his firm's important clients, a man with whom Walter had had many dealings, came to visit the factory and was entertained, but Walter was not invited.

Now there was no doubt in his mind that his days at the firm were numbered. He became morose, stayed away from his friends, and spent most of his free time watching television. His wife, Elaine, tried in vain to convince him that he was not reading the signs correctly, that surely there must have been other explanations for what was going on. She is a vivacious, outgoing person, who is generally optimistic, and although Walter appreciated her efforts, they did not convince him.

However, when Elaine noticed that Walter was losing interest in sex, and that the few attempts he made were unsuccessful, she began to think that he was ill. She urged him to have a medical checkup. Typically, when he went to the doctor he withheld the most pertinent information, his impotence. He felt that if there was something wrong with him the doctor would find out. But the doctor found him in excellent health. Elaine could not believe this verdict and begged him to see another doctor. This time Walter felt impelled to reveal the shameful truth. The second doctor, also unable to find anything wrong with him, thought he might be overworking and suggested a rest. Walter duly requested a week's leave of absence from his firm for health reasons, was granted it, and took off for a resort. But he felt so miserable there, missing his wife, not seeing his children, and not knowing what was going on in the firm, that after a few days he returned home and immediately went back to the second doctor. This time, seeing the intense agitation breaking through Walter's self-control, the doctor referred him for psychiatric consultation.

Walter's predicament is typical for a large number of young men in our midst, especially those who show great promise and are considered on all sides to be on the way to good careers. When a person puts all his resources into the pursuit of a single goal, he enhances his chances of gaining it but at the same time he becomes more vulnerable to any setback. With everything he is, and has, concentrated in one direction, any reverse is more of a stress to him than to one whose aims are more diverse or whose existing achievement is less. Under the strain of the setback, even if it is only an imagined one, there is a gradual erosion of the brain's capacity to reason, at least in that sector that affects his career. As the stress heightens, panic sets in, and the sequence we have described is set into motion. The body's responses become subject to the emotions, the second level of the brain, and eventually to the third one, the automatic reflexes. At this level there is an exact duplication of what happens in any higher group animal in the rest of nature. The messages received from the brain by the hormones spell out defeat, and the body reacts with all the appropriate mechanisms. Having lost rank and with it the privileges of mating, his sense organs and glands become unresponsive to the lure of the female. That this effect is an inestimable advantage to the harmony of a herd is obvious. But man cannot live with such an arrangement. His neocortex constantly reminds him of his expectation of being a winner even while his body is reacting as if he were a loser. Thus, the one significant system that is peculiar to man, his ability to reason, in such instances is responsible for many of the psychological ills that befall him. Fortunately, reason is a two-edged tool. Just as it can interfere with a natural process it can also point the way out of the conflict.

The Search for Degradation

Having made a case for the importance of a sense of status in natural sexuality, we now come to practices that would seem to controvert everything we have so far written: those that are often referred to as "sexual perversions." These practices plainly involve feelings opposite to status, since humiliation, degradation, and pain are used as fillips to sexual excitement.

How does a sense of status come into the picture when a man hires a girl to whip him to orgasm or when a woman is excited by the kind of physical abuse that is parodied in an Apache dance? Obviously it does not. Such behavior has nothing to do with the sexuality that governs the formation of breeding couples and ensures that those creatures that are born and reared have the best chance to be fit members of their societies. What, then, is the difference between this kind of stimulation to sexuality and the "feeling good" about oneself that is the essence of status?

The first thing to recognize about this kind of sexuality is that it has nothing whatever to do with reproduction. It has to do with people who have difficulty experiencing emotional responses and who can arouse feelings in themselves only by bombarding their senses with what for others would be excessive stimulation.

There is, however, one sensation that does not allow itself to be turned off entirely, and that one is pain. If, by some chance, pain becomes associated with a sexual experience early in life, later on it is only possible for that person to respond sexually if there is an accompaniment of pain. Some people who have been subjected to severe whipping on the buttocks in childhood are later only able to respond in this way. Not a few have reported that after the first sensation of extreme pain there was a pleasurable sensation of warmth that had a sensuous quality for them. As adults, then, the sex, as it were, rides piggyback on the pain into the person's awareness.

The reasons for such people's inability to experience a normal quota of feelings lie in their early lives. We can understand this best if we think of the numbing of feelings any one of us suffers as a result of a shock. A dulling of the senses is the brain's way of protecting itself from emotional turbulence, and when any child is in a situation where its daily experiences are shocking, then its feelings become numbed. Thus it suffers less and is enabled to carry on its life unaffected by the shocking circumstances. The penalty such a child pays for this protection, however, is that its feelings may be turned off to such an extent that it becomes unable to experience the normal sensations of life, including the pleasurable ones. As it grows up it hears others speak of excitements and pleasures it does not feel.

One young man whose mother was given to hysterical outbursts managed to grow up without too much distress by completely shutting off all his responses to them. In the process he cut himself away from emotional involvements of any kind. He was a good boy. He was dutiful and did everything that was expected of him. It was only when he reached the age of twenty and became involved in a homosexual relationship that anyone in his family realized he had ever had any problems at all. In conversation this boy spontaneously expressed his opinion that displays of love, joy, anger, and the like were a kind of acting, or, in his word, "phony." Unable to relate to women because of his deep fear of the hysterical outbursts he associated with them, he turned to his homosexual relationship in an effort to try to experience those sensations of love and pleasure that he had heard his friends discuss. Although in this relationship he experienced at least the physiological evidence of excitement, he was unable to experience accompanying emotion even here. He found himself being an observer of his own actions and not an emotional participant in his relationship, and this, in fact, brought the relationship to an early end.

Another young man with a similar background (except that both his parents were hysterical) was mystified as to the reasons why people smile. He figured out in his mind that it must be a part of a speech pattern, and he tried to copy it, sometimes with rather odd results. That a smile is a natural expression of pleasure never occurred to him. Needless to say, he had sexual difficulties.

If one can make a distinction between mind and body, then degradation is to the mind what pain is to the body. Both hurt, and it is open to opinion which hurt is the greater. Therefore there is a great deal of similarity in the backgrounds of those who seek degradation and those who seek pain in order to experience sexuality. The greater the wall they have put up between themselves and sensation, the greater the degree of degradation they must seek in order to achieve sexual satisfaction.

The degradations sought are as varied as the imagination can conjure up. Being urinated or defecated upon are among the more usual. Some men, who need both physical and mental pain, pay women to walk on them with spiked heels.

In people whose feelings are partially shut off, an awareness that there could be more creates a frustration, which drives them to search almost compulsively for means to intensify the sensations they are capable of. This results in the whole range of behavior that comes into the category of sexual perversions: from death-defying pursuits to abysmal humiliations, torture and mutilation either of the self or of others, thrill murders, all the way to the least extreme derivatives.

Because of their extreme drama, these cases find their way into the literature more than their proportion in the population warrants. We have also to bear in mind that some deviations are a result of external circumstances rather than of character structure. Homosexuality in a prison population is a consequence of the segregation of the inmates and not necessarily a reflection of their bent; incest and bestiality in rural areas can be a result of the absence of human social contact more than of a desire for either of these sexual outlets.

We once made an excursion in the region of Foum el Hassan in the south of Morocco in the company of our friend Boris Witjas, who is a doctor of medicine by profession but an archaeologist by avocation. Near Tirherc, in an area that shows records of a transition from a hunting to a herding culture, he drew our attention to rock carvings he had discovered and that have been identified as late neolithic. One of them gives an explicit illustration of bestiality. Of course, the orthodox interpretation of such carvings is that they represent a rite or an element of a rite. On the other hand, knowing as we do of the customary obligation of a groom to present a bride's father with valuable gifts before a marriage can take place, we could suggest that the rock carving depicts either a man who was too poor (unsuccessful) to obtain a bride or one whose status was so low that he was relegated to guarding herds in outlying places (a task that is usually assigned to children) and therefore had no other outlet for his sexuality.

To those moralists who attribute deviance to the ill effects of civilization and who advocate a return to a more pristine way of life, we feel that this carving and others like it at Tiouet in Tunisia and at Ojerat in Egypt, dating back to neolithic times, afford a telling proof that no culture of man is entirely simple.

Selective Impotence

A quirk that is distinctly human, and here again the mind plays a large part in it, is an impotence that selects its targets. It affects men and women equally, and it may be exercised in one of two directions.

Animal sexuality is chiefly governed by two factors: hormonal condition and rank. In human beings the hormonal condition is less decisive, but rank remains. For some men and women sexual relationships are only possible with partners of lower rank, while only partners of higher rank spark the interest of others. The mind's role in this sexual oddity is in judging the rank of the prospective partner.

A businessman may find himself incompetent with women of his own social circle, and especially with his wife, but filled with desire for a waitress who serves him lunch. A society woman may feel total sexual indifference for her husband and his like, but feel ardor for a beach boy she meets by chance on vacation.

This man feels, and therefore is, inadequate with women of his own station, but feels like a king toward the waitress who scurries to the kitchen at his command, brings him what he orders, and seems crestfallen if he should appear unpleased by her services.

The woman, too, may feel inadequate with her husband, even if to the onlooker theirs looks like an ideal partnership. We knew a young woman who was a great beauty and who at the age of nineteen made a socially very advantageous marriage to a handsome young man of twenty-seven who was wealthy, intelligent, capable, and of good social standing. Four years later she abandoned husband, home, and a young child and acted out a literary cliché by running away with their chauffeur. What went wrong?

This young woman had been brought up by an adoring mother who told her from the time she was a baby how pretty she was, how any man would eat out of her hand when she was grown up, and how she would always be able to have what she wanted and do as she pleased. By any definition her mother spoiled her and at the same time gave her a totally false picture of life. When she married, her husband indeed adored her. He gave her plenty of money to run their home, servants to help her, beautiful clothes, and whatever she needed. But he had certain expectations of her. He wanted her to look lovely all the time, not just when she went out; he wanted his home run beautifully and his friends entertained elegantly. He wanted more than the ornament her mother had brought her up to be. He wanted a functioning, effective mate and partner, and she did not feel capable of this. Handsome, wealthy, and desirable as her husband was, her feelings shut off toward him but glowed again when the chauffeur made his admiration plain. To the chauffeur she could be once again the ornament, the shining star. Nothing was required of her; she could be comfortable, even proud, of what she was, and all her responses were ignited.

Selective impotence also can work in the other direction. Some men and women who are particularly capable, alert, and ambitious and who by all the laws of nature should be functioning automatically at top capacity in all areas may find themselves totally cold and disinterested toward partners of lower standing. Here the judgmental qualities of the mind are the arbiters of sexuality. For those whose aspirations keep their sights high, only partners of superior rank are interesting and therefore stimulating. This is not solely a peculiarity of the social climber. A man whose passion is bowling but whose wife's is not may find her dull; but the women champion of his bowling club will seem enormously attractive to him.

None of the people who exhibit selective incapacity either in an upward or in a downward direction could be described as biologically impotent, yet in effect there are partners with whom they are unable or unwilling to function. Rarely for a woman, but sometimes for a man, this creates a problem, especially in those who can function down but not up. A woman will tell herself simply, "This man appeals to me and that man does not. I am hard to please" (and perhaps consider this to be a virtue). A man of the same type may be afraid of his wife's criticism or fear that something is wrong with him and seek help. But when he finds the waitress, or whoever she may be, who fans the flame of his ardor, he may then reassure himself and attribute his lack of desire for his wife to a dearth of attractive qualities in her. The other man, who is only excited by women of superior status, can only be described as selectively impotent if we include an attitude of disinterest or coldness as a phase on a gradient of the phenomenon. Such a man or woman is left cold by others below their own rank. If they see a necessity to do so, they can bring themselves to function with anyone, but their total responses are only engaged by higher rank, and to this extent their sexuality may be described as limited.

It is tempting to look on such sexual selectivity as the particular whims of individual personalities, but selectivity is far from this. It is the example *par excellence* of the social basis of sexual responses for, although the judgment of what constitutes rank in each case is individual, that judgment is based on a perception and awareness of social factors.

The False Appearance of Dominance

There are some occasions, perhaps not so rare as some of us think, when a person who to all outward appearances is successful, nevertheless exhibits behavior that we would associate with a "loser" or unsuccessful person. We read in the newspapers of well-known personalities caught in acts of sexual deviation, which seem to contradict everything one might expect in the behavior of a successful person. But the private feelings of such people that might make their actions understandable never reach the newspapers. Where we do have more information, the picture becomes clearer. Two striking examples occur to us.

The first was an English dealer in fine arts. By any objective standard he was a successful man. His gallery, which had been founded by his grandfather, under his direction continued to attract the cultural and industrial elite of many nations, and he was apparently on terms of friendship with most of them. His home was in some ways an extension of his gallery. Its contents were magnificent, and there was no doubt that his financial resources were on a par with its splendor. Yet this man was unmarried, and there had never been the slightest involvement in his life, either heterosexual or homosexual, that those who knew him were aware of. It was only through the indiscretion, or perhaps the spite, of an employee that a few people learned it had been his practice to disappear to Jamaica at times when it was believed that he was on an art-buying trip. There he frequented an establishment that provided men of his bent with black female children below the age of puberty.

When one learned of this, the occasional incongruities one had noticed about the man began to fall into place. His public personality and the few visible facets of his private personality were poles apart. With his sophisticated clients he was worldliness personified, and yet in the company of his brother and his brother's friends he was painfully shy. Obviously the image of success and high standing he presented to the public did not coincide with the way he felt about himself. He was a short man, blond-complected, mild-mannered, and bald. Perhaps his lack of self-confidence as a male stemmed from these facts, or perhaps from things that it was not possible for an outsider to know. Whatever the causes, his acts were those of a man with an inner feeling that he was not attractive to women in spite of his prestige. The children he consorted with obeyed him (they would have been punished had they not) and the darkness of their skin released him from the feeling that he was involved with a female of his own kind.

The second was an American in his late forties. He was vice-president of a well-known bank, and he had all the outward accoutrements of success: a town apartment at a good address, a country home, membership in a good country club. His marriage, however, was not at all happy. He and his wife had separate bedrooms, and he had not entered hers nor she his for several years. One day his wife made a discovery that so shook her that she flew to a psychiatrist for advice. Chance had taken her to her husband's room in response to a maid's query about linen. Not knowing that he was in (he normally was in his office at that time), she had not stopped to knock. When she entered his back was turned toward her, and he had not yet put on his shirt. She was stunned to see his body covered with raw welts, as though he had recently been lashed. She cried out, "What in the world has happened to you?" He turned round unsteadily, plainly still intoxicated, and mumbled, "It's none of your goddamn business." Then, irritated, he added, "If you really want to know I was over in Jersey at my whorehouse last night and—get out of here!"

That evening, when he was sober, she tried to get more from him, and he admitted that it was a craving of his from time to time to be beaten. She was so horrified that she didn't know what to say or think. All she could understand was that he must be mentally ill, and she suggested he ought to see a psychiatrist, but he refused. She then took it upon herself to make the visit.

She told his story: his father, now retired, had been chairman of the board and to a large extent responsible for the bank's success. Her husband was never quite able to follow in his father's footsteps. He had been expelled from several schools and barely managed to earn his degree from a minor college. Without his father's influence he could never have held on to his job at the bank, as on occasions he showed up for work slightly drunk. He was able to hold his liquor, and so it was not obvious to most of the personnel, but his associates were aware of his state. In spite of his large salary he was always short of money. She didn't know what he did with it, only that his mother always made contributions to the running of their household.

She was advised that she should persuade him to obtain professional help, and she did this by threatening to tell his mother if he did not. When he entered the office he stated, "I don't know what I'm doing here. There's nothing wrong with my head. Can't a man have a little fun without all this fuss? After all, I pay for it—and I don't deduct it from my taxes! And if you want to know, you should come with me one evening—it would be an eye-opener for you. You'll meet an abridged edition of *Who's Who* there." He maintained this attitude for the few minutes he remained. Then as he left, not making use of his allotted hour, he said, "Well, thank you, doctor. I don't want to take up any more of your time. Send the bill to my wife." He never returned.

This man was another example of how easy it is to be misled by external appearances. By any standards he would be thought of as the archetype of success. He was in an esteemed profession, his social standing was first rate, he was a respected member of the Episcopal church, he contributed to many charities, and he was the son of a founding member of his country club. His sexual habits, on the other hand, spelled out LOSER in capital letters: one who deliberately seeks humiliation and pain. Such a state of affairs would contradict our thesis had we not heard the story from his wife, and probably no one else ever saw the whole situation in its true light.

These men are but two of a large number of men and women like them whose success, though seen and sometimes envied by the world, is no more than a veneer covering insecure personalities. These people could not have achieved their high positions by themselves. When we know more about their careers we usually find that their families or social backgrounds have placed them in their high positions, and their education has often given them the means to sustain places that their native wits could not have achieved for them unaided.

There are other successful people who have all the attributes of winners. Whether born to high position or not, they would have found their winner's niche at any level of society. Even these people, however, are not immune to private fears. Some may be made to feel insecure by maneuverings within their organizations, others by the fear of a change of direction in their field that might make their positions redundant or untenable. Then there is a third group, who, because of their very eminence, are constantly subject to challenge. This applies to the champion prizefighter, the star athlete, the great actor or actress, the successful labor organizer, the political or social leader, as well as the corporation executive, the fashion designer, the university president, the acclaimed scientist, or singer, or the police chief. These people hold their positions by force of their skills and personalities, and as long as they retain those strengths they hold their places. In this they are like the dominant stag who holds the leadership of his herd so long as he is able to defend it: as soon as he weakens, ever so slightly, there are many waiting to challenge him for his place.

To such men and women a temporary fear of downfall is not unknown. After all, as the Chinese say, "the higher a man climbs the more you can see of his arse," and few who have reached heights do not at moments experience at least passing thoughts of their increased vulnerability.

Some people have a buoyant self-confidence that shows itself by many signs. Their glands being always at the ready, they seem to be almost tireless. They enjoy their work and are perpetually active. Should they be presented with leisure time they will fill it with one or another form of purposeful activity: public service, charitable projects, study, research, the development of new ideas or of new approaches to old ones. People of this type do not panic when they see danger signs on the horizon. They make plans to shift into allied occupations or to try their skills at new ones. They are resourceful, and in one way or another they manage to cope with stress. Nonetheless, such men and women are still human beings, an animal species, and subject to the forces that are built into life. While their absence of inner panic saves them from the temporary bouts of impotence suffered by their less confident brothers and sisters, they experience a preliminary phase of it: a lack of interest in the opposite sex, an absence of desire.

This feeling is not usually recognized for what it is. In an animal with a less highly developed neocortex than ours a shutting off of the sex drive can be prompted by two types of experience: loss of rank and danger. In man, whose body responds to the interpretations his mind puts on events, we have to add to these the thought or idea that a threat to status may arise or that a situation may have dangerous elements. To the person who is not securely dominant the possibility of a change in his circumstances may seem to presage eventual loss of rank, and this feeling promotes bodily responses that may lead to impotence. The securely dominant person, however, sensing danger ahead, merely responds as any animal does and suppresses any activity that is not immediately concerned with meeting that danger and mastering it. The sex drive is irrelevant to coping with danger, and it is shut off. But as soon as the danger is dealt with—avoided, mitigated, or turned into new mastery—the self-confident individual makes a rapid return to normal function.

The secure person obviously does not think of what his body is doing in these terms. His own view of himself is that he is busy, his thoughts and plans preoccupy him, he falls asleep still contemplating courses of action. But when his course is set to his satisfaction his mind, free again, will permit the reemergence of his less essential activities.

For the less secure person, on the other hand, the indifference to sex promoted by worry about the future is actually the first manifestation of eventual temporary impotence. It can be thought of as the first of the series of reactions that leads to the ultimate elimination of the defeated animal from the ranks of the contestants for dominance.

We are reminded of the reactions of two of our acquaintances of some ten years ago, who showed the differences we are speaking of very clearly in their behavior.

Raoul, a Frenchman in his early thirties, was an engineer who specialized in the design of suspension bridges. He was extremely talented, and his work was sufficiently known and appreciated for him to be invited to join an American firm. He was a bachelor, the idea of experience abroad before settling down appealed to him, and he accepted. Raoul advanced rapidly in the American firm, and it was not long before he was fully in charge of the department concerned with designing bridges. He had ample funds and was able to indulge freely in his private talents as a ladies' man. No matter when one stopped by his apartment to pay him a visit, it was always decorated with the presence of attractive young women. But though Raoul's course looked as if it was headed into easy sailing for the rest of his life, it began to encounter squalls with the development of sophisticated computers. As he explained it later, there are not too many variables in the design of a suspension bridge. A basic program fed into a computer and modified only by such factors as the width of the river, the height of its banks, the number of traffic lanes it is to carry, and the like, will produce a satisfactory result.

Raoul's firm was a large and rich one, and it was one of the first to buy and use computers for designing purposes. Raoul himself had charge of them and of their programming, but he saw the writing on the wall. His whole special field was becoming superfluous, and this worried him. All that we and his other friends knew at that time was that he was no longer available for parties, and he was unaccountably often found alone in his apartment. It was only when we ran into him sometime later that he told us about the problem he had faced and the difficult decision he had had to make: whether to move to a smaller, computerless firm, return to France, try a new field. By the time we met him his decision had been made. He was engaged in highway design, and he had a lovely young woman on his arm.

Raoul's behavior was characteristic of the naturally dominant members of a group in any species. When problems or challenges arise they devote the full power of all their energies to dealing with them and then rebound, with no more backward glances. They are concerned with the future and not the past. In sociology's jargon we could describe them as "future-oriented."

But what about the person who has all the appearance of dominance, but who does not feel secure in some area of his existence?

We once crossed paths with the works manager of a small paper goods factory, whose experience will tell the story for us. He had left home young, but his speech revealed his Highland origin, and his workmen called him Scottie. He had been barely fifteen when his father was killed in an accident, and he had gone south to try to earn a living and help his family. When he began to make a little headway he invited his younger brother to join him, and a few years later they sent for the youngest boy too. When all three of them were earning enough to keep themselves with a little to spare, they pooled their resources and asked their mother to come and keep house for them.

Scottie had started out as a general helper on the lowest level. He swept up, tidied, made tea for the others in their work breaks, and made himself generally useful, all the while learning what he could about the operation of the machines. When a position opened up to help on one of the machines, he asked to be given a trial and was taken on. Industrious and conscientious as he was, over a period of time he advanced to become a foreman, and in that position he truly bloomed. He felt on top of his job. He knew all there was to know about his machines, and he was popular with his men, who did their best under his direction.

So well did he do that management took an interest in him and tried to groom him for a higher position. They gave him manuals to study, and this was where his inner problems started. On the one hand he was grateful for their confidence in him and he was ambitious enough to want to justify it, but on the other his educational background was insufficient, and he had the utmost difficulty in understanding the material he was given. In practical matters he was in control, but when it came to grasping theory and mechanical principles his struggles were Herculean. But somehow he managed, and when the old works manager retired he was given the job.

To all appearances here was a successful man. The administrative departments relied on him completely, and he remained well liked and esteemed by his men. Only his wife had an inkling of what it cost him. She saw him change from a patently happy man into a more and more morose one, even while he did not let a glimmer of this appear to anyone else. If you had told any of his men that he did not feel sure of himself they would have laughed in your face. But he began to suffer from headaches severe enough to send him to a doctor, who found also that his blood pressure was unduly high. Moreover, ever since his promotion he had lost interest in sex. Fortunately his wife, busy as she was with three young children, didn't complain. In his own mind, he blamed his headaches.

At this stage we can see the difference between Scottie and Raoul. Had Raoul been faced with a complication of his work that he felt was beyond his competence, he would have taken one of two courses. Either he would have put all his energies into it until he indeed mastered it, or he would have said, "That work is not for me," and turned his attention to an alternative field. Scottie had great personal strengths, but not quite enough for that. He was grateful to his employers and wanted to please them, and he couldn't face losing the position he had achieved. So he spent his days in fear of downfall. To outsiders he was a man who had made the grade, but in his own feelings he had stepped beyond the limits of his capacity. This caused inner tensions that were manifested in his bodily functioning. In Scottie we can see the paradox of a man who is accepted as a leader or as successful in his field but who nevertheless has sexual problems.

We have written of Raoul and Scottie because their experiences so clearly illustrate our point, but today when women are engaged in competitive fields, they are subject to the same feelings and responses. Even women whose lives are led in purely domestic occupations can face parallel situations. A woman who has spent many years building up a home and a place in her community and is faced with a radical change in her way of life can also react like Raoul or like Scottie. If she is of truly dominant fiber she will devote all her energies to making the necessary change in the best way possible. While she is so preoccupied her husband will probably find her less compliant or available than customarily, and he will probably have occasion to tell their children,

"Don't bother your mother, she is busy," or, "She has a lot on her mind at the moment." But when she has things worked out to her satisfaction she will soon return to her normal competence in all areas. A less self-assured woman may suffer indispositions, headaches, and more permanent changes of mood that will inevitably find their way into her sexual life.

Conversely, a person may seem to us to be of low rank, or functioning on a lowly level, but may feel himself or herself to be important. An outsider cannot tell what sustains the self-esteem of such people. It may be that they have found a niche for themselves in which they feel supremely confident or merely that they enjoy the respect of their families because of some physical attributes (muscular strength, skill at a game, a fine voice, or whatever). An outstanding farmhand given different circumstances and education in his youth would have turned out to be an equally outstanding lawyer, teacher, or businessman. There is a quality about these people, and it is personal—we would almost call it glandular—that predestines them to do well in any field to which they find their way. On the other hand a person may be esteemed in his work but demeaned at home, and this will be reflected, too, in a reverse response.

The Successful Person Who Abstains from Sex

If we assume that natural mammalian (and avian) sexuality, operating through the hormonal apparatus, has evolved as a mechanism for affording care to the young through the bonding of a male and a female, then we may say that the bonding is the aim of the prolonged, or heightened, sexual process. The end, bonding, is more important than the means of achieving it. When you have a creature that can give care as a result of alternative mechanisms (by cerebral resolution, for example), then this means will also be manifested.

Man is the first creature on the evolutionary tree of life who is able to achieve a bonding by other than sexual means. Men and women are able to experience a sense of dedication, to give care and devotion, in every way comparable to a parent's, through the exercise of will.

Thus a priest, for example, sacrifices only the copulatory aspect of sexuality. He is bonded to the church and, though giving up personal fatherhood, takes on the duties of father to his flock. A Florence Nightingale is bonded to an ideal, and her family comprises all the wounded and sick. An unmarried principal of a school likewise takes on family duties with all the attendant feelings of responsibility and care.

The personal circumstances of the lives of these people have precluded the conventional form of bonding, marriage. What these circumstances happen to be will be as varied as the people who have chosen to remain single. But even if such persons do not engage in copulatory activity, they are still sexual beings. It is not unknown for priests to leave their orders and marry. If they were successful as priests they are probably potent husbands. Unsuccessful priests leaving their orders would find the same sexual problems as any other losers. Indeed, we knew a case of a novitiate who couldn't make it as a priest and later couldn't make the grade as a lover either. On the other hand, the medieval tales of licentiousness among priests and nuns do not prove anything except that they were men and women like everyone else.

Gandhi, in his autobiography, acknowledged himself to be an extremely sexual person. His later asceticism was undertaken by deliberate act of will to free himself from all entanglements that might distract him in the slightest degree from the supreme undertaking of his life.

In the (apparent) absence of copulatory activity, whether of the priest, the political or social leader, the spinster or bachelor school principal, or any other person dedicating himself to the care of others or to a cause, we cannot *prove* that they are not devoid of passion. But in those instances where such persons are later presented with opportunities for conventional sexual expression, it is our experience that their competence in this area parallels their achievements in their previously chosen fields.

The Shy Person

There are cultures in which modesty is a virtue. The greater the man the more likely he is to downplay his own achievement and give credit to the work of others. Boastfulness is the cardinal sin, and the person possessing healthy self-esteem learns to cover it under a cloak of socially acceptable self-deprecation.

In a culture of this kind it is the privilege of the society to judge the worth of the person and not the right of the person to assess himself. A student may not say, for example, "I have an interesting case to present to you." The professor will admonish him, "You have a case to present. We will decide whether or not it is interesting." Not that the student may not boast with impunity about some inconsequential accomplishments, usually in the area of flirting or drinking, but as soon as his achievement is serious, boastfulness is taboo.

Where social conventions of this sort exist, it is easy for a person's shyness to be camouflaged in the general aura of modesty. He may be particularly appreciated by others as a fine, worthwhile colleague who does not push himself forward. But the shy person's feeling about himself is light years away from the conventional modesty of demeanor exacted by such a group. The conventionally modest person, while observing the behavior expected of him, is confident in his own abilities. The shy person, on the other hand, usually has highly exaggerated ideas about what is expected of him, and he has the feeling that he will seem foolish if he is not able to live up to these ideas. He cannot enter a room and make casual conversation, because he feels that what he might say would not be interesting enough, whereas the more confident person knows all that is called for is a friendly "good morning" or "good afternoon." He makes these random remarks without giving them a second thought and without the least notion that he will be judged on his performance. To the shy, though, it seems that the public will judge him on the basis of such inanities, and, above all, he prejudges them himself. He tells himself that he is sure to make a fool of himself, that he will make some blunder ("put his foot in it") and feel dreadful. Because of this, social encounters are so painful to him that he does what he can to avoid them.

Surprisingly enough, although the shy person would be the very last to see it, much less acknowledge it, he is the most competitive of all. Every "hello" he utters is in competition with all those unseen others who surely say it more cheerfully, pronounce it more correctly, convey more friendliness in it, than he believes he is able to do. In effect he puts himself into competition with the whole world, all the time, and tells himself that he has lost, before he does anything at all. He then experiences the physical loss of buoyancy, the pain of losing, exactly as if he had indeed been challenged and found wanting.

This kind of person, in self-protection, is often to be found functioning in some walk of life that is far below his actual ability. He is likely to bury himself either in a very large organization where he can remain inconspicuous or to engage in private occupations like the arts or sciences where he can work alone.

A shy person, left to his (or her) own devices, would usually remain unmarried but, being inclined to be nonassertive, may find himself involved in a commitment through his efforts not to displease. Men or women of this kind are then usually dominated by their mates and spend a lifetime suffering the indignities that come their way, little realizing that in many ways they invite the criticism they are afraid of. Were they more self-assertive they would not provide such easy targets.

It goes without saying that sometimes two shy people find each other and experience great comfort in each other's presence and love for each other. Ideally they then often retire into a private world of their own, but if circumstances force them out into the competitive world they may well take refuge in excessive drinking to bolster their social confidence.

In our general thinking we have no conception of shyness as in any way an illness. Shy people do not show up for treatment in doctors' offices unless secondary problems take them there, and yet they suffer constant tortures. Where services are available, such as a clergyman's or the counseling services provided by many schools and universities, they do not use them, not wanting to expose themselves.

The French playwrights Robert de Flers and G.-A. de Gaillauet in discussing their play *Monsieur Brotonneau* in an interview for the Paris newspaper *Figaro* (March 19, 1923) intuitively seemed to know this, and they put their collective finger right on it. They are quoted as saying:

"Ils vivent—c'est-à-dire ils suffrent—naturellement. Et ils ne font pas appeler des docteurs en psychologie, tellement leur vie, c'est-à-dire leur souffrance, leur semble naturelle."

(They live—that is to say they suffer—naturally. So much does their life—that is to say their suffering—seem natural to them that they do not call for [the help of] psychiatrists.)

Yet if we look at this problem squarely we can see that it is in its essence a byproduct of the status mechanism, for it involves a person's image of himself vis-à-vis others. But it is a byproduct that is out of kilter. A degree of distortion of the useful mechanism is involved, and as a result the effects are all awry. The distortion exists first in that no competition actually takes place, and second in that the result of the nonevent is predetermined.

By far the most usual victim of this kind of shyness is the teen-age girl who has no confidence that she is pretty. When her friends give a party she cannot be persuaded to go. All she can imagine is that the other girls will be invited to dance, but that she will be left without a partner and not know what to do with herself. Unaware of what she is doing, she is actually measuring herself against the as yet unseen crowd, and nothing anyone tells her can change her private judgment of her chances in it.

Some less shy people can sometimes be helped by a change of environment. A young person who has grown up convinced of the inferiority of her social charm to that of the girls with whom she was raised may blossom when, as a newcomer in a strange place, she finds other people interested in her. A man who is awkward and unsure of himself at home quite often blooms abroad, where he may feel that all his judges were left behind and that in the new place he is free.

Since nature offers a gamut, there is a variation on this variation. It is the manic state, in which an individual's sense of competition is unbridled by any modification of reality. He feels that he is the best in any field he hoes, that he will surely win any contest he enters, that no one else is as good as he. But while this, too, is also a distortion of the status drive that regulates our groups, it is a condition, or state of mind, that arises from an abnormal disturbance of the brain.

15

Turning Losers into Winners

The sense of status is as much a part of our lives as the air we breathe; most of the time we are not conscious of its presence. As we only notice the air when something is wrong with it, when pollution makes us choke or dims its clarity, so we usually only become aware of our own sense of status when something infringes it.

So important is our sense of status that to feel demeaned, even remotely, can have consequences that may range from the most obvious show of hurt pride to inexplicable behavior or symptoms of poor health that are difficult to connect with the offense that set them into motion. When a person is insulted and reacts with anger, the cause and effect are easy to understand, but when an apparently healthy woman suffers from fatigue, insomnia, and a general listlessness, it is more difficult to connect these symptoms with her attitude toward her overly patronizing husband. Even more remote are signs of stress like hypertension or chronic indigestion from the feeling that a business partner, say, does not appreciate a man's contribution to a firm. We even find a lowered resistance to disease in those who feel downgraded or who only fear the possibility that they may become downgraded. It has been shown repeatedly that students anticipating difficult examinations are more vulnerable to respiratory tract infections than they are at other times of the year.

When we realize how all pervasive to our general sense of well-being is the satisfaction of our status needs, we can see how important it is to find solutions for any disturbance of them.

Fortunately, this is not beyond the bounds of possibility. There are few absolutes in nature, and it has been found that even the most rigid social groupings among animals do not preclude a certain amount of social mobility. About six years ago it was reported that in a group of baboons studied closely over a period of several years, a few individuals had been able to advance their standing within its hierarchy in spite of the strict and definable order that was readily apparent at all times.

Scientists recording the social dominance patterns in a herd of cows came to the same conclusion. They stated that although there was *no* interaction between any two of the animals that was not modified by the relative rank of each, nevertheless there was a small percentage of animals whose relative position in the ranking order changed during the period of observation. They particularly noted that dominant members of a new generation were able to make their way upward within the established order without disrupting it.

We might note in passing that the social dominance patterns among cows and hens, and many another agglomeration of female animals, has exactly the same significance as it has among male animals. Habits of speech and thoughts about "dominant males" sometimes tend to make us forget this. Vance Packard tells an amusing anecdote of when he was a farm boy in northern Pennsylvania and his father pointed out to him that one of their eighteen cows, whose name was Gertrude, always came first through the gate at feeding time. Later he observed that another, rather rusty cow almost always came last and that, in fact, each animal seemed to know its proper place in the lineup. When Packard's father bought a new cow who butted her way to the top spot within an hour after entering the barnyard, Gertrude "developed neurotic symptoms and became the meanest kicker at milking time."

If it is possible for the comparatively rigid structures of animal groups to be modified by self-assertive newcomers or by crises of self-doubt in established members, then how much easier it must be for man, in his more fluid social groups, to improve his standing.

By now we have made it plain that some of the world's success stories from humble origins to great wealth or power (like Napoleon) are not examples of rising rank in our sense. Such people had great confidence in themselves, and in fact had status, even in their early days. We are now talking of those of us who experience self-doubts, lack self-confidence, are inhibited from striving, and feel like social losers.

When we use the word *loser,* in fact, we are making no reference to the objective values of any particular culture. We would not automatically call a street sweeper a social loser nor a millionaire a winner. We are using these terms purely as they apply to the biological mechanism that we find operative within us and that manifests itself through our feeling that the world is our oyster (the feeling of the winner), or that whatever we do is too great an effort, cannot be successful, or has no meaning for us (the feeling of a loser).

In order to give help to a loser, there are one or two fundamentals to keep in mind.

Pitfalls

First, as we have been at pains to show, one of the most inevitable areas where feelings of lack of personal worth make themselves known is the sexual area. In young people this may express itself in a reluctance to go out and meet other young people; in the mature it may be seen in a falling off of sexual interest; in the elderly it may appear as a waning of sexual powers. Above all it is necessary to recognize that these are secondary manifestations. Not only is it not helpful to discuss the sexual problem or to focus attention on it in any way, but to do so may actually be harmful insofar as it will tend to increase the person's existing feelings of inferiority.

The second pitfall is the attitude of the would-be helper. An habitual underdog stance in any member of a family is apt to generate one of two responses in the rest. One is a feeling of general impatience along the lines of, "Come on, now, pull up your socks and get going," and the other is an oversympathetic attitude. The first tone of voice cannot possibly be helpful. The insecure person knows exactly what he ought to be doing and does not find himself able to do it. Impatience in those around him can only increase his sense of frustration.

The overly sympathetic approach accomplishes even less. It reinforces the sufferer's sense of helplessness and sometimes makes him completely dependent on his well-wisher, a fact that can only intensify his feeling of low status. This particular pitfall accounts for the largest number of failures in patients who seek psychotherapy, irrespective of the school. Ironically, in seeing themselves in a subordinate role to the kindly and all-knowing therapist, the patients can never free themselves of the condition for which they seek help.

The most subtle pitfall of all is love. Countless understanding wives who love their husbands and who would do anything in the world to help them are dismayed to discover that nothing they do is helpful. There are women who have studied every book on the psychiatric shelf, informed themselves of all kinds of physical means of stimulation in efforts to arouse their husbands, all without result. The same is true of loving husbands in the reverse case. *Potency is not a derivative of love so much as of a feeling of confidence in the self.*

There are three important phases in turning around a person's feelings about his own social worth. The first may be called *identification.* It is the phase in which a person comes to recognize the source of his difficulties. The second phase is *evaluation.* In it a judgment must be made whether the problems exist in reality or only in the mind of the sufferer: whether the difficulty is actual or only one of interpretation. The last is to find the way by which the loser may be enabled to see his status in a more positive light, either by reevaluating his situation in his own mind or, as is sometimes possible, by changing his external circumstances in some way so that he feels more comfortable.

Phase One: Identification

It would seem logical that if a person is suffering because of the way he is being treated by others, he would be aware of it. But human personality being constructed as it is, this is usually not the case. On the contrary, it is quite rare for a troubled person to be able to identify the source of his difficulties. His all-encompassing need is to preserve his pride, and to do this he will usually find all kinds of legitimate-sounding reasons to account for his state.

The chief unease that concerns this person is that he feels generally low. He has no energy and everything he does seems to cost him unreasonable effort. He feels that he is not performing to the best of his ability. He knows that he can do better, but he doesn't seem to be able to bring himself to get down to things or to work up any enthusiasm for anything. He will probably tell himself, or his family, if they are prepared to listen, that he needs a tonic, that he is a bit run down. Feeling tired all the time, he will probably remember that it is a long time since he took a holiday. He may complain that he seems to need more sleep these days, that he doesn't sleep as deeply as he used to, that little worries play on his mind.

If our man goes to a doctor with this set of complaints the doctor must look for a disease that these symptoms reflect, and there are a few. He will check for anemia, low blood pressure, or possibly the first signs of some chronic disease. Not long ago, if he couldn't find a basis in any of these, a doctor might have blamed a vitamin deficiency or a low-grade virus infection, although there was really no indication of the existence of either. There is a tendency to hang the complaints on the few hooks that are available and can accommodate them. But if one separates those people who really have these diseases from the huge numbers who complain of the symptoms we just described, the proportion is infinitesimally small.

Today, on the whole, there is a greater readiness to recognize in such symptoms the signs of a low-grade depression. But, having said that, what in fact have we said? We have put a label on the condition, but the label is neither a cure for it, nor even a real understanding of it. It permits treatment with antidepressant drugs, which may alleviate the symptoms for so long as they are taken, but no drug can change the circumstances that caused the person to become depressed.

One indication of the number of people afflicted with mild depression is given by the huge sales volume of over-the-counter remedies and the vast advertising programs that promote them. No company could stay in business for long if huge numbers of people did not identify in themselves the conditions these products claim to cure: indigestion, headache, insomnia, tension, "tired blood," irregularity, and so on. Any one of these conditions may well be an aspect of "depression."

There is such a great distance between the event that causes a loss of status and the eventual bodily symptoms that develop as a result, that it is perhaps not so surprising after all that a depressed person often fails to recognize the true cause for his state.

To give an idea of how difficult it sometimes is to identify the status problem as the source of a psychosomatic disorder, let us look at a typical sufferer of chronic headaches.

Quite apart from possible physical causes, there are many possible emotional reasons for chronic headaches. Any strong feeling that is suppressed, especially anger, may well find expression in this way, but the chances are better than even that where you have constant headaches that seem to be incapable of relief, you have a person who in some way is suffering from an injured sense of status.

By far the greatest number of headache sufferers, from all causes, are women. And one of the reasons that it is so very difficult to discern the element of denigration in these instances is that on the whole, objectively, the women are well treated. A woman herself will often volunteer the information that her husband is very considerate and that they have a good relationship. This woman is usually an intelligent person. She fulfills the role that society assigns to her and is a capable housewife, but this occupation by no means exhausts her capacities. She knows there are many other things she could do, and often she wishes she had an opportunity to do them. What is particularly galling to her is that her husband shows his appreciation of her domestic skills and "feminine" qualities and often praises her for them, but constantly downplays her understanding of other matters, making remarks like, "You wouldn't know about that," or "Don't get into that, dear, it's really a man's job."

This general attitude may display itself in some quite trivial ways. If the couple are bridge players, for instance, when they arrange to have a game with friends the husband will invariably be placed in the "man's game," which is presumed to be the better one, even if his wife happens to play far better than he. She will be expected to take a place at the table of weaker players and to be pleasant about doing so.

This woman has a constant feeling that she is being made to seem less important and of less value than she inwardly feels herself to be. But this feeling has to be tightly corked, first because she probably loves her husband and doesn't want to spoil their marriage, second because she does not want to appear ungrateful, and third and above all because she herself does not fully connect up in her mind what she thinks of as these constant petty irritations and the painful headaches that she suffers.

The thick wall that most people put up between their conscious thoughts and awareness of their injured self-esteem makes direct questioning useless. If you were to ask a woman like this if she were angry at her husband, she would point out that she has a very good marriage and that she and her husband understand each other very well. The only way to get at the root of any discrepancy is to engage her in a casual conversation about what her aspirations were when she was younger, what her dreams are still, or what, if she were given a chance, she would most like to be doing right now. Out of this a picture will emerge that shows very clearly the gap between her dreams and her present reality, and in the process she herself will become aware of it.

If you now explain to her that whenever a strong desire or a drive of any kind is blocked, it is a perfectly normal reaction to feel frustrated or angry, the implications will become plain to her. If one blocks feelings of anger in one's head, one will experience a headache; if the anger is blocked in the chest one will have a "tight feeling" there and difficulty in breathing; and if the anger is blocked in the stomach it will reveal itself as indigestion.

Now the big question is, with whom is she really angry? Is she angry with her husband because he assumes a role of male superiority and treats her like a little girl? Or is she angry with herself for allowing this to have happened? Having permitted herself to be pushed into a subordinate role, she reacted like a subordinate creature. As such, she had no real fight left in her, because subordinate creatures don't fight back. In retrospect she couldn't be angry with her husband for doing what came naturally to him, because she never called his attention to it, and she couldn't be angry with herself because once she accepted the subordinate position there was nothing left for her to do but nurse her headache!

Phase Two: Evaluation

In the second phase the chief objective is to discover whether this woman is actually capable of leading the kind of life she dreams about or whether her dreams are just idle fantasies. The easiest way to do this is to find out how she uses her free time. If her aspirations are intellectual, has she kept up her reading in her field of interest? Has she kept her mind stimulated by cultural pursuits? Has she undertaken voluntary commitments from time to time? Usually men or women of the type in our example begin many things but, not having the winning streak, do not follow through. But there are also those whose ambitions are just pipe dreams. Their most frequent word is *if:* "If only I had had the opportunity. . . ," "If only I had been able to travel. . . ," "If I had a knowledge of languages. . . ." But *if* such people are presented with opportunities, they usually let them slide by. There is always a good reason.

To help these two kinds of people, you have to use different approaches.

Phase Three: Finding a New Way

Let us take first of all the woman who has let herself get painted into a corner. She actually has the background and interests that would enable her to do more with her life, but she never insisted on her right to time to pursue anything outside her home and gradually she has lost her initiative, her "get-up-and-go." She has fallen into habits of spreading out her household tasks and just being available to her husband for the rest of the time.

Granted that she realizes all this now, really knows with her deepest feelings that it is true, then this is not the time for kindness. Something has to spark her into changing her self-defeating pattern, and sometimes the best way is a challenge, even a challenge with a suggestion of doubt in it. "Perhaps you have good reason for not wanting to put your abilities to the test? Are you really sure you could handle such a radical change? After all, it's not so easy to take on an unaccustomed new role."

By talking to her in this way you are repeating her own doubts back to her. You are actually stealing her script, but having somebody else play it back to her produces a very predictable response: almost invariably an angry rebuttal. This is exactly the anger that earlier would have been directed inward against herself and, suppressed, was the cause of her headaches. At this stage the challenge is usually sufficient to light the spark. What she does from then on depends upon circumstances. She may make false starts and experience setbacks, but it is the beginning of the undoing of the spirit of the loser.

What about the person whose secret aspirations are in truth pipe dreams? This person too has a general dissatisfaction with her life, and often thinks that if only some aspect of it had been a little different she would be a much happier person. But her dreams are not realistic, and in her heart she knows that she is not really able to be other than she is.

The first thing necessary to help such a person is to understand what in her life causes her to dream those idle dreams of glory.

This kind of self-delusion is most likely to happen in a woman who, at the time of her marriage or during her married life, moved away from her original environment. She feels that she would have found acceptance easily where she grew up within the circle of her family. Away from her home and family connections she has to find her own level, and here her difficulties could begin. Those women who have a strong sense of their own worth will find their level wherever they go and lead contented lives, but those who do not will perpetually feel slightly insecure in their new surroundings, and sometimes the feeling of insecurity will mount with time. In the new place she will meet other women from different backgrounds whose ideas are at variance with her own, and she may find some of the axioms of her existence shaken. Not having the inner resources to cope with this, she protects herself as well as she can by telling herself that if this or that had happened, or were to happen now, she would be like these new women she meets.

To reduce this situation to its social and biological essentials, she finds herself in competition with women of her new circle. Unlike our previous example, who is in competition with both men and women and wants to be accepted on equal terms, this wife is competing (as other creatures do) only with the members of her own sex. But she finds herself outclassed. She finds other women more sophisticated then she, they look more elegant to her, they know more. Their homes seem more impressive, their conversation leaves her feeling slightly stupid. If, added to this, she then has a growing suspicion that her husband finds these new women more attractive, she will probably feel cool toward him. This will only intensify her already low interest in their sexual life, which in turn will add its quota to their deteriorating relationship.

Such a woman will experience a rising sense of anger which, in her case, is clearly directed toward her husband, but she will not dare to express it openly for fear of losing him. She does not have confidence in her ability to manage on her own, and so the anger she feels is an additional threat to her, adding to her insecurity. She blocks it, and in the process becomes a sufferer of headaches.

To bolster what little self-esteem remains to her, she then indulges in daydreams: if she had a job that took her out into the world she would get along just as well as her husband; if she could find the time to attend a course at the local college she would be the equal of any of those women; she'd do it if only she didn't have those awful head-aches, and so on.

It is far more difficult to turn around the feelings of such a person than our earlier example, who has some resources of personality and ability on which it is possible to focus. In this case we are dealing with a person who is by any definition a loser, and as such she has been edged to the periphery of her group.

At this point one thing is plain: she has become an invalid. Her headaches have become so incapacitating that her family is convinced there must be an organic cause for them. She will be sent to a doctor or a clinic and will receive the customary checkup. These examinations, some of which are painful, will convince her that she is indeed a sick person. If she is fortunate the doctors will find nothing wrong with her. But if by chance some minor abnormality is found it will be treated, and she will be doomed to being an invalid for the rest of her life, because it has no relevance to the real source of her headaches. But in the best circumstance, when no abnormality is found after repeated tests, she will eventually be sent for psychological examination.

At this stage there has to be an evaluation. Has the process gone too far? Has she been reduced to a nonfunctioning entity? The pitfalls to be avoided, if this is the case, are sending her to a hospital and giving her lengthy insight therapy of any kind. Either course can only increase her sense of being an invalid. In the hospital she is relieved of all responsibility, and she has a face-saving excuse for not confronting her own inadequacies. With the psychotherapist she will live in an island of unreality and become dependent upon him. The best thing one could do for her would be to send her back to her parental home, provided that it is a warm and supportive one. There she will be removed from the toxic environment that caused her condition, and she will be accepted and feel adequate. She will then slowly regain her former sense of status. Once this is accomplished it forms a fresh base upon which one can attempt to build anew. She has ceased to be a loser, although she is by no means ready to return to her husband. It is now that one can talk to her about what her hopes had been when she was young.

Being from a traditional background, in all probability she will say, "Getting married and having children, just like anybody else." This is something one can get hold of. It provides an opening wedge. One can ask her, "When you were young (and had self-confidence) did the women you know seem to be contented with their lives?" Should she affirm that their lives were fulfilled, which they surely were, we can now face her with the disparity. She has achieved her hopes. She has married and had children. What went wrong?

The chances are that she will bring up her health, and the headaches. She must be persuaded not to think about her headaches for a little while, but to talk about what she thinks would happen to any girl from her family who might have been transplanted into the same circle of new people as she had been. With a little prompting she will say that the girl would feel alien, unaccepted, awkward, and not able to join in their pastimes—golf, tennis, card games, or whatever they are—while it would be much easier for the girl's husband to get along with them because of his professional connections and mutual interests. In talking about this hypothetical other girl, she will come to see her own predicament.

Nevertheless, it will still not be easy sailing. From time to time she will continue to insist that the headache is the overriding complication, but eventually she will come to realize that she had set herself an impossible goal in attempting to compete with women whose backgrounds were so different from her own. Surely she could find some women closer to her own kind among the mothers of her children's school friends, in a church group, or in a garden club, depending upon her bent. This is her own responsibility. No one else can do it for her. Besides this she will come to see that there are differences between people that she must recognize: that the people with whom she was unable to mix were neither necessarily better than she, nor worse, just different; that a truck, for example, cannot be driven so fast as a racing car, but that there are many occasions when a truck is much more useful than a racing car, and who can say which has the greater value?—and so it is among people.

Ideally, if all goes well, she will now rouse herself to find new friends who have interests on a level with her own, and in doing so she will find that there is no necessity for her to be sophisticated, an intellectual, a clotheshorse, or anything else that she is not, and that there is no special virtue in any of these qualities. If she can follow through along these lines she will no longer feel defeated. On the contrary, she will have a sense of rank, and her headaches will be less and less frequent.

This sounds very easy, but in fact it is a tough, uphill struggle. In the end its success will depend upon the kind of resources a person has left. For the woman we have talked about, who had a good home life, one could predict a good outcome. But for a person in a similar situation who had had an emotionally crippling childhood, the way back is much more difficult, though not impossible.

What we try to do with this approach is to recognize the responses to which we all are heir because of our evolutionary past and because these responses are still prompted by our old brain. Recognition of the responses is achieved with the highest processes of our new brain, and by the agency of the new brain, too, we try to turn around our old responses and use them to our advantage. With our new brain we recognize the existence of mechanisms that have regulated groups from time immemorial, including a basic striving for rank and an automatic giving up when it is not achieved. With our new brain, however, we can redefine what we mean by achievement. If we cannot succeed by one set of conventions we can try again with another set. This possibility is not open to other species. They must stand or fall by the conventions to which they were born. But we may look at the rule book in any number of ways, and sooner or later we shall find a way in which it is possible for us to compete on our own terms and to have a chance to succeed.

With this ability to redefine the rules we live by, we can block the defeat mechanism. If we can see opportunity in another area or in another way of looking at the same area, our glands start discharging hormones at an optimal rate again, where before they inhibited them. We have discussed the powerful influence of the mind over bodily responses, and this is the most powerful of all. Where the mind sees defeat, the body experiences it, but where the mind sees opportunity and the possibility of new contest, the body recharges itself for the fray.

With this in mind let us look at the youngster whose problems about sexual identity mark him as one with a sense of defeat.

When we are dealing with adolescents or young adults, there is no question but that their glands are at the ready. It is extremely rare to find in them problems that impede their glandular function, except in the minute percentage of cases with congenital abnormalities or with the disabling consequences of certain diseases. When difficulties arise in members of this age group they are almost invariably connected with the strength of their own conviction of their sexual identity, with their evaluation of themselves as members of the new orders of manhood and womanhood that they are about to enter.

Most young people slide into these roles by degrees with only minor upsets and readjustments along the way. The adolescent with a good sense of self-confidence will go through a period of trial and error but come out at the other end with a feeling of being adult without having to be instructed about his or her role. This has been the pattern throughout human history, and on the whole it has worked. Where the roles of the parents are clearly displayed as models throughout the growing period of the young, no problems usually arise.

But in those young people who evaluate themselves as being ill prepared to enter adulthood, we see behavior that indicates this inner feeling. Any social situation that they feel calls for an adult response, such as meeting a member of the opposite sex and behaving appropriately, fills them with discomfort so disabling that any attempt to pressure the youngster into social participation may make him feel physically ill. It sometimes happens that before or after, or even more embarrassingly during, a social engagement that has been imposed by the parents, the excessively shy boy or girl may vomit or suffer an attack of diarrhea.

It is very rare for an adolescent to be able to explain what is beneath this kind of response, but here and there one finds a youngster with the perception to realize that what is feared is the certainty of appearing foolish and being exposed to ridicule.

By the time we are adult it is hard to remember the agonies that this fear evoked in most of us at one time or another when we were young. But if we remind ourselves that scorn and ridicule by the peer group are the weapons used by any tribal society to remove its inadequate members from the center of its life, we can realize their importance. Ridicule, in fact, is the weapon by which any person can be made to feel less. It is the supreme tool of the basic human group in organizing its hierarchical structure. Moreover, we can readily observe it at work in any group of very young children, who reflect in much of their spontaneous behavior the habits of preliterate tribal communities.

Over a period of four years' observation of a group of children aged from three to five, we ourselves noted these mechanisms at work. We have already described the emerging leaders, but there was also inevitably a "fall guy." For a period of almost a year this unfortunate child was a girl named Deanie. She was included in all the children's games but invariably was assigned the part of scapegoat, bad man, victim, or whatever role was the unpopular one in that particular game. Whenever you heard a child call out "Bang, bang, you're dead" in a game of Indians, you could count on it that Deanie was the one who was expected to lie down and play dead. We never had a chance to discover what was the quality in Deanie that caused the other children to assign this role to her, because the child became so unhappy that her parents removed her from the group, but there is no doubt in our minds that Deanie felt herself in some way to be less than the others, and that this feeling communicated itself to them.

If we transpose this kind of behavior to a higher age group, this assignment of the low role to certain individuals is the equivalent of ridicule. Traditionally the defeated warrior has been assigned menial tasks or displayed and subjected to the scorn of the populace. The French army custom of publicly ripping off the insignia of rank from the shoulders of a disgraced officer and drumming him out of his regiment in the presence of all is the supreme symbol of the vestiges of these ancient practices among us. Even today, United States pilots who have been brought down over North Vietnam have been demeaned by being paraded through a town, stripped of their martial uniforms and the trappings of power, and exposed to public contempt.

The abysmal feeling set up by this kind of treatment is very deeply embedded in our response mechanisms, and it is to the fear of just this sort of treatment that the adolescent responds if he is not confident in his ability to take on his approaching role. He anticipates and fears public shame.

Since nearly all teen-agers have normal glandular function, their sex drives are intact. It is the mating, or rather the bonding, drive that is impaired by their fears. This shows itself in excessive shyness, in not wanting to expose themselves to their contemporaries, in shutting themselves in their rooms, daydreaming, engaging in solitary pursuits, in either masturbating excessively or developing a morbid fear about masturbation, or in homosexuality if they find a kindred soul. All of these are in fact makeshift solutions attempted by the young people to find an outlet for their needs. But we can never emphasize strongly enough that all or any of them are secondary to the prime cause: the sense of inadequacy and the fear of shame.

We stress this so strongly because in most cases, when parents troubled about the social problems of their sons and daughters take them for treatment, it is the manifestation that holds the eye of their attention and not the underlying fear. This has most unfortunate consequences, because the young person feels new demands being made on him while the source of his difficulty is not being removed. He was not able to meet society's expectations of him in the first place, and now he feels that his burden is becoming greater and his ability to carry it less.

If we keep in front of our mind's eye the model of the animal that does not challenge the leader of its group because it senses that it stands no chance, then we can see that to put social responsibilities on these young people is to place an undue stress on them. It is as though we were to expect a short, fat, totally nonathletic person to take a place in the lineup for an Olympic race. He doesn't stand a chance, and he knows it. To make him participate is to subject him to the humiliation of being laughed off the field.

The very first thing we have to do if we want to help this young person is to relieve him of the pressure. We have to make him know without any shadow of doubt that we expect absolutely nothing of him that he doesn't feel comfortable about doing; that he has no need to feel guilty about not fulfilling his parents' hopes for him, nor for not pleasing his doctor by getting better; that we only want him to feel more comfortable, and everyone concerned will be happy about that.

Once this is accomplished, and he actually feels that it is so and not just a trick of the kind he has certainly experienced in the past (well-meant deceptions, when he has been told that he is going to visit relatives and that no one else will be there, but when he arrives he finds a young woman present with whom he has to make conversation, and similar maneuvers), then, as casually as possible, the subject of his special accomplishments may be brought up for discussion.

He may have a good collection of records; he may play an instrument, collect stamps or other items; or he may simply be a round-the-clock watcher of television. Once we convince him that what he is doing is not a waste of time (which he has probably been told a thousand times), but that his pursuit has merit that probably only a very few people recognize, we have got his foot on the first step.

At first he will disbelieve us. We may then point out to him that a variety of professionals are paid to do nothing else but watch television. Some are technicians, some monitor commercials, and so on.

One would mention to a collector that any kind of collection can be a serious business; that people go to all kinds of lengths and expenses to complete collections of any objects in which they may be interested. To the solitary guitar strummer we mention that many great minds find relaxation in music.

The purpose of all this is to elevate his pursuits into something more important in his own mind than he had been led to believe or than he himself thought. This boosting must be tempered with moderation. It will not help him to suggest that in collecting he is becoming an expert in a certain field, that his television watching may be a step on a path leading to his becoming a great performer, or that his strumming will turn him into a gifted musician. To do this would be once again to face him with high expectations that he feels he could not fulfill, and he might give up even that modicum of interest that he shows.

One day then we ask the television addict, for instance, what he thinks of certain commercials, and he will offer an opinion. Then we may ask him if he could watch the commercials for the purpose of writing down his opinions, as if he were a critic. This is a task he is accustomed to, so it doesn't alarm him, but a new element has been added: we are asking his opinion. In time, without fail, he will begin to offer his opinion about what he has seen. We may then casually ask his opinion about other aspects of television or other programs. Surprisingly, or perhaps not so surprisingly, we shall probably hear some very sound views. The time will come when we may mention to him that we find his views original and ask him if he ever thought of discussing them with members of his family.

Now we have his foot on the second rung, because we have convinced him that he has opinions and that they are worthwhile listening to. Being able to express those opinions, even if only to members of his own family, is step number three: he has something of merit to tell others.

Step number four will take place when his family, and he himself, will see him as an expert, for now he can compete in an area where he has a good chance to win because he knows more about it than anyone else present.

If we observe him when he reaches this stage we shall notice that he is more alive when his particular subject comes up for discussion;

he will offer opinions; every so often his statements may be set forth with an air of authority.

This is the time when one can ask him whether he has ever thought of offering his opinions to people other than his family. One can suggest that quite a number of people would be interested in his views. And now a little manipulation is in order. Some people may be invited to the house who have been asked in advance to express interest in his subject and requested to pose questions that will draw the young man into conversation. With this, it will slowly dawn on him that a topic of conversation in which he feels very secure can engage almost anybody's attention.

It is then only a question of time before he will *voluntarily* test himself by making a date with someone of the opposite sex. The rest, now that he can lead from strength, will be just a question of experimentation. The only thing that could set him back at any stage along this line is undue prodding. For this approach to be successful it is essential for expectations to be kept realistically low, even below his actual abilities, the whole way.

As one can see, it is a painstakingly slow process, and one must know in advance that there are no shortcuts. To turn a convinced loser into one who has enough confidence to be willing to compete is literally the resuscitation of an individual from the brink of social death, and it can only be achieved small stage by small stage.

The same basic principle applies to helping a depressed old person. In this case the person is not starting out with the idea that he has nothing to offer, but that whatever he had to offer is over, and that no further function remains to him. In his case also it is necessary to rebuild his confidence that there are indeed areas in which he can contribute, and no one else so well as he, and then to give him the opportunity to prove this by putting it into practice, step by slow step.

There is another set of conditions that poses more of a philosophical question than a psychological one. We can exemplify it best in the case of a family where the father has an undemanding position as a minor civil servant and is perfectly happy in his role. He is not an ambitious person. His real passion in life is puttering around in his garden, where he raises dahlias. In this area he is extremely knowledgeable: he has produced some splendid specimens, and he exhibits regularly at the local horticultural club shows. As long as his job provides him with the wherewithal to pursue this hobby, he is perfectly contented. After about ten years of marriage, the mother in this family took on a job in the local library. It is not a very demanding occupation, but it suits her purposes very well. It helps her to supplement the family income and at the same time gives her a little interest outside their home.

This couple has one son, a totally noncompetitive spirit. He is quite content to help his parents out a little around the house and garden. After he left school he tried his hand at one or two jobs but could not adapt himself to the nine-to-five discipline and did not much like taking orders. He then settled into taking small commissions for an antique dealer who was a friend of his father's. He made photographs of pieces that the dealer wished to show to distant clients, and sometimes he took smaller pieces for sale among his own acquaintances on a commission. He was able to conduct this little enterprise very comfortably from his home, where he was not subject to any office discipline and could perform his tasks as and when he pleased. Often, if he had nothing particular to do, he didn't get up until noontime, but no one reproached him. His parents are quite happy to have him around the house. They have equipped one room for him as an office. He does small chores for them while they are working and otherwise spends a great deal of time watching television.

This boy functions sexually and socially perfectly satisfactorily. In his own small niche he can by no means regard himself as a loser, no matter what the opinions of the larger community may be, and therefore he shows no objective signs of the person without status. Unlike those who cannot live up to their parents' expectations, he is not depressed, not angry. On the contrary, he is an amiable young man. He has a number of friends and some gratifying relationships with girls. He seems able to find young women who are not demanding of him and who, rather, are often able to help him out with connections for possible sales. He is a pleasant fellow, and they accept him for what he is, in much the same way as his parents do.

What if a well-meaning outsider, say a successful relative, descends upon this family, points out that the boy is being encouraged in lazy ways, that the parents are irresponsible, asks what will happen to the son when the parents are no longer around to provide for him, and asserts that the boy would be perfectly capable of working like anyone else if he were forced to, but if things go on the way they are he will become totally unfit for normal life?

What this relative cannot see—nor, for that matter, can the society of which the boy is a part—is that the reason he is functioning as well as he does is that no pressures of any sort are being put upon him either by his parents, his friends, or his style of life, and that so long as this set of conditions is undisturbed he will continue to function adequately.

But let us suppose that one day, against his own precautionary feelings, this boy allows himself to be persuaded that he would like to get married. We can foresee that with the prospect of responsibilities and the pressure of having to earn enough money to contribute to the support of a household, he will begin to show signs of stress. Not long after he marries he is going to become uncomfortable and unhappy. Not knowing the reason, he will start to find fault with his wife. He will blame her for the absence of a hundred and one little things that he was accustomed to and that she is not providing or doing. The wife will try to please him in any way she can think of, but when all fails she will probably consult her mother and other relatives, who will surely tell her that what her marriage needs is a baby.

This, of course, is the worst possible advice. If he continues to live near his parents or his wife's parents, he will somehow be able to manage. He will continue to take help from them as he has all his life, and he may then regard his infant as the one positive achievement he has been able to attain. His parents, though, cannot be there to support him forever. It is far more likely that the arrival of the baby will be the last straw on the pile of pressures that his marriage puts on his shoulders. If, as is likely, he is devoid of a bonding drive, his child will seem to him a squalling interloper who disrupts his sleep, takes up the time and energy of his wife that should be devoted to him, and has insatiable needs. He will begin to stay away from home whenever possible. He may get into a habit of hanging around a bar or of playing cards or dice late into the night. His sexual drive will diminish, since it has become associated with the responsibilities of marriage and a child and is no longer the pure gratification it was earlier. This lack of interest is only a short step from partial, and eventually total, impotence.

Now that we see the problem whole, how shall we view the intervention of the well-meaning outsider who, after all, represents society's views? Does he perform a useful service or does he stir up a hornet's nest? The first question is whether this young man should not be left alone to function at his own level. If he should not be left in his Eden, but be forced to embark on the course that leads him to greater effort, and to failure, the second question arises: what is now the appropriate measure?

Suppose the second course has been taken and the young man is induced by other well-meaning friends to seek treatment for his impotence (or homosexuality or pedophilism or whatever path his difficulties lead him to). What should be the aim of the individual who is delegated to help him? Obviously the sexual difficulty is but a fraction of the total picture. It is quite clear that he should never have married, but since he did, is he to be left to make himself and two other people unhappy? Can he be helped to function as society expects him, or should he be guided back to the level of function that is within his power to sustain, even if it involves breaking up his marriage?

Before we can answer such questions, we have to face some very difficult philosophical problems about the perfectibility of man. Does one accept limitations and live within them? Does one believe that every human being can be made into the equal of the most gifted by the expenditure of unlimited resources of science, wealth, and insight? If one believes this, does one also believe that it is in the best interest of the individual that it should be done? Last, but not least, what is the role of the helper? Is he the agent of society or the servant of the individual? There is no consensus here. The therapist, having no guidelines, has to struggle with thoughts like these in every case. The most positive thing one can say is that so long as one's goals are limited, it is possible to succeed in attaining them. Later, as one goes along, one may judge whether it is feasible to raise the goals.

As we have seen throughout this work, sexual function, and indeed general function, follow closely on a person's feeling about his status. But this is a basic concept. For each person who has no sense of status or who has a firm feeling that his standing in relation to others is irremediably low, there will be a set of circumstances that are special to him or to her. To be able to help him turn these feelings around until he can feel comfortable in some form of competitive existence, no matter how minimal, an approach has to be devised for each individual personality. The approach must take into consideration the particular hook that the person's low feelings are hung upon; the circumstances of his life that caused them to be so low; his present circumstances; and the realistic possibilities that are still open to him.

In some cases, where the person has a reasonably good sense of self-esteem, all that is necessary is a change of environment that can be achieved by job counseling, and results may be speedy. In others the task is uphill and arduous, as we have described. And then there are all the gradations, combinations, and permutations in between.

We should not like to give the impression that lack of a sense of status, alone, is responsible for all dysfunctions. It has been our purpose to draw attention to status because it is probably by far the most prevalent, and certainly the most overlooked, element of individual dysfunction in our society.

We cannot overlook those people who suffer from a form of the crises of survival, which may in some cases show itself as a mild anxiety but in others may amount to a terror of life coming to an abrupt end. This often accompanies organic disease, but it includes some special fears like that of flying in an airplane, suffocating in an elevator, or drowning. Nor can we overlook those whose lives are sometimes dominated by crises of separation, which include the fear of loss of someone close. The loss itself when it comes is then overwhelming and often heralds deep depression. This sense of loss and its resulting depression are different from the depression that is a result of loss of rank. The latter case involves much anger that is absent in the other.

There is no question that these two other types of crisis are clearly distinct from the loss of rank. Much attention has already been given to them, and they have been widely studied, as have what are generally termed the psychoses: those severe mental illnesses in which perception and judgment are impaired.

But, granting the existence of difficulties, discomforts, and diseases based on these other crises, there remain thousands of people who can be helped by keeping the model of a natural hierarchy in the forefront of one's mind. It was Shakespeare who observed that there are "tongues in trees, books in the running brooks, sermons in stones," and we should like to add this other lesson that can be learned from nature herself in the marvelous order that exists in all species and the potential for change and development that derives from it. Most higher animal species perpetuate themselves by restricting reproduction to those animals that feel themselves to be dominant. Together with their social status goes sexual drive, mating and breeding rights, and all the competitive aggressiveness necessary to sustain these functions. Animal species also maintain their fitness by eliminating nondominant individuals from the ranks of their breeders, and this is effected in an orderly way by the inhibition of sexual drive and the turning off of aggressiveness in the subordinate.

We are heirs to these mechanisms. But we are also the possessors of a brain that may define a situation differently in different individuals. By the use of this brain we may often be able to find an alternative niche in which a person may feel comfortable and of sufficient status, even if he feels uncomfortable and of low rank in the one in which we find him.

It is not necessary for a human being to be confined, or to confine himself, permanently to a status of low rank. If we wish, and if we believe it to be useful, we may transform almost any of our losers into winners.

Sources

Beilharz, R. G., and Cox, D. F. "Social Dominance in Swine." *Animal Behavior* 15 (1967):117–22.

Bettelheim, Bruno. *Symbolic Wounds: Puberty Rites and the Envious Male.* New York: Collier, 1962.

Buckner, H. T. "The Transvestite Career Path." *Psychiatry* 33 (1970):381.

Carr, Donald E. *The Deadly Fest of Life.* London: William Heinemann Ltd., 1972.

Carr-Saunders, Sir Alexander. *The Population Problem.* Oxford: Clarendon Press, 1922.

Cooper, Alan J. "Understanding Impotence." *Psychiatry,* special publication of *Medical World News.* New York, 1972.

Crowcroft, P. "Notes on the Behavior of Shrews." *Behavior* 8:63–80.

Devereux, George. "Institutionalized Homosexuality of Mohave Indians." *Human Biology* 9 (1937):498–527.

Dilger, W. C. "The Comparative Ethology of the African Parrot Genus *Agapornia,*" *Zeitschrift für Tierpsychologie* 17 (June 1960):649–85.

Ellis, Havelock. *Psychology of Sex.* New York: Emerson Books, 1945.

Freud, Sigmund. *The Standard Edition of the Complete Psychological Works of Sigmund Freud,* translated by James Strachey. London: Hogarth Press, 1956.

Gebhard, P. H., et al. *Sex Offenders.* New York: Harper & Row, 1965.

Genesis 29:20.

Gilliard, E. T. "Bower Ornamentation versus Plumage Characters in Bower-birds." *Auk* 73:450.

Guillemin, Roger, and Burgus, Roger. "The Hormones of the Hypothalamus." *Scientific American* 227:5 (November 1972).

Harlow, H. F., and Harlow, M. K. "The Maternal Affectional System of

Rhesus Monkeys." In H. L. Rheingold, ed., *Maternal Behavior in Mammals*. New York: Wiley, 1963.

Hingston, R. W. G. *The Meaning of Animal Colour and Adornment*. London: Edward Arnold & Co., 1933.

Hubbard, David. *The Skyjackers: Flights of Fancy*. New York: Macmillan, 1971.

Imanishi, K. "Japanese Macaques." *Psychologia* 1 (1957):47.

Jay, Phyllis. "Indian Langurs." In I. deVore, ed., *Primate Behavior*. New York: Holt, Rinehart & Winston, 1965.

Jonas, David, and Jonas, Doris (Klein). *Man-Child*. New York: McGraw-Hill, 1970.

———. "The Price of Pride." *World Medicine*. London, November 1973.

———. "The Evolutionary Roots of Some Psychosomatic Ailments." Paper read at 1st Congress of the International College of Psychosomatic Medicine, Guadalajara, December 1971.

Kardiner, A. *The Psychological Frontiers of Society*. New York: Columbia University Press, 1945.

Karlen, Arno. *Sexuality and Homosexuality*. New York: Norton, 1971.

I Kings 11:3.

Kinimouth, C. *Morocco*. London: Cape, 1972.

Lang, H., and Chapin, J. P. "Notes on the Distribution and Ecology of Central African Chiroptera." *Bulletin of the American Museum of Natural History* 37:98–108.

Lindsay, D. R. "Mating Behavior of Ewes and Its Effect on Mating Efficiency." *Animal Behavior* 14 (1966):419–24.

MacLean, Paul D. Address delivered at the scientific symposium held during the sesquicentennial of the Institute of Living, Hartford, Connecticut, May 1972.

Marshall, A. J. *Bower Birds*. New York: Oxford University Press, 1954.

Mead, Margaret. *Male and Female*. New York: William Morrow, 1949.

Medical World News. Report on testosterone levels in relation to social status. March 31, 1972.

———. Report on "How the Brain Rules the Hormones" 13:40 (October 27, 1972).

Mitchell, Alexander, and Miller, Russell. "Idi Amin." *The Sunday Times Magazine*, London, October 29, 1972.

Noble, G. K. "Sexual Selection Among Fishes." *Biological Revue* 13:133–58.

Packard, Vance. *The Status Seekers*. New York: McKay, 1959.

Payne, Robert. *The Life and Death of Adolf Hitler*. New York: Praeger, 1973.

Pearse, A. S. "Habits of Fiddler Crabs." Annual Report for 1913, 415–28, Smithsonian Institution, Washington.

Peters, H. F. *My Sister, My Spouse: A Biography of Lou Andreas-Salomé.* New York: Norton, 1962.

Price, John. "The Dominance Hierarchy and the Evolution of Mental Illness." *Lancet* 2 (July 1967):243–46.

Richards, Christina M. "The Inhibition of Growth in Crowded *Rana pipiens.*" *Physiological Zoology* 31:138–51. As cited in V. C. Wynne-Edwards, *Animal Dispersion,* Edinburgh: Oliver & Boyd, 1962.

Robertson, D. R. Report on sexual transformation of *Labroides diminiatus.* In *Science,* as reported in *Time,* October 30, 1972.

Roheim, Geza. "Psychoanalysis and Anthropology." *Psychoanalysis and the Social Sciences.* Vol. 1, International Universities Press, 1947.

———. "The Oedipus Complex, Magic and Culture." In Vol. 2, above.

Rowell, T. E. "Hierarchy in the Organization of a Captive Baboon Group." *Animal Behavior* 14 (1966):430–43.

Salzman, Leon. "Changing Styles in Psychiatric Syndromes." *Psychiatric Spectator.* Sandoz, New Jersey: October 1972.

Shakespeare, William. *As You Like It.* 2, l. 12.

Suetonius. *The Twelve Caesars,* trans. Robert Graves. London: Penguin Books, 1957.

Tardieu, A. A. *Etude Medico-Legale sur les Attentats aux Moeurs.* Paris: J. B. Bailliere, 1857.

Time, December 1, 1972, p. 39.

Wagnon, K. A., et al. "Social Dominance in a Herd of Angus, Hereford, and Shorthorn Cows." *Animal Behavior* 14 (1966):474–79.

Wendt, Herbert. *The Sex Life of Animals.* New York: Simon & Schuster, 1965.

Wynne-Edwards, V. C. *Animal Dispersion in Relation to Social Behavior.* Edinburgh: Oliver & Boyd, 1962.

Zilborg, Gregory. "Masculine and Feminine." *Psychiatry* 7 (1944):251–90.

Index

About the Authors

DORIS JONAS and DAVID JONAS are American citizens living in London. Doris Jonas is a fellow of the Royal Anthropological Institute of Great Britain. For many years she was director of the Department of Anthropology at the Institute of Theoretical Medicine in New York. David Jonas practiced psychiatry for twenty years in New York, where he was also director of the Department of Medicine and Psychiatry at the Institute of Theoretical Medicine. He now teaches at St. Bartholomew's School of Medicine, London.

The Jonases have been group and family therapy leaders and marriage counselors and have based this book on the case histories of persons who were helped by their methods. Their previous works include *Man-Child, Other Senses, Other Worlds,* and *Young Till We Die,* as well as numerous articles for professional journals.